TEACHING MIME

ROSE BRUFORD

HON. R.A.M.

FOUNDER OF THE ROSE BRUFORD
COLLEGE OF SPEECH AND DRAMA

London
METHUEN & CO. LTD
11 New Fetter Lane, E.C.4

First published July 31, 1958
Reprinted 1960, 1964 and 1966
Reprinted with corrections 1969

1·5
SBN 416 60320 3

Distributed in the USA
by Barnes & Noble Inc

CONTENTS

PREFACE TO
FIRST EDITION

I have written this short text-book, hoping it will help the many teachers who have asked me to do so. The book sets out to guide these teachers, and others who want to make a beginning in mime. I hope, however, that they will add and develop their own ideas, using this simply as a starting point, so that their work does not become static and limited.

I would like to acknowledge kind assistance from my colleague, Greta Stevens, who has worked with such meticulous care on the proof reading of this book. Also to express gratitude to Helga Burgess for her advice and help, and to Jay Vernon, whose research has contributed much to the historical section of Chapter X.

I wish also to remember and thank Irene Mawer for her wonderful mime classes from which I learned so much when I was a student, and since then at her inspiring vacation courses, and I must also mention the work of Michel Saint-Denis whose artistry and teaching has always been a source of inspiration to me.

Barbara Lander's musical compositions, which are being published in a separate volume,[1] are an integral part of this book, and students and teachers who know her gift of

[1] *Music for Mime,* Methuen

improvisation will be grateful, as I am, for her collaboration. Her book provides music for most of the examples needing accompaniment in this book, as well as for several of the Mime Plays in Chapter XIII.

I wish to thank Edith Scorer, and my brother, Lionel Bruford, for their constructive ideas, their kind patience and their continuous encouragement.

I am deeply grateful to Mr A. E. Dean, C.B.E., M.A., (formerly Warden of Goldsmiths' College) for so kindly writing a Foreword for me. During his retirement Mr Dean has given generously of his enthusiasm, his experience, and his great wisdom, and has been of the utmost help in developing the Education Department of the Rose Bruford Training College; I am proud that he is now one of its Governors.

Dr John Masefield, O.M. has specially written a poem to open this book, remembering the day in 1951 when he first visited the College in Lamorbey Park and saw some mime. I am very much aware of the honour he has done me, and thank him for his friendly and untiring help and guidance at all times over a long period of years.

Rose E. Bruford

It is with sadness I record that many of those who inspired me to write this book are no longer with us, but my gratitude will always remain.

R.E.B., 1969

FOREWORD

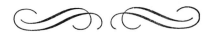

This is a book primarily for teachers and should be of great value, both to specialists and in ordinary classroom work, not only for the copious variety of the suggested practical exercises, but also for the thoughtful theory concentrated on these. It is not an easy book, for it sets its sights high, e.g. in Chapters IV and VIII, and in the last three chapters.

Miss Bruford is herself a fine teacher of great experience, and a fine teacher of teachers. For the last five years I have watched with admiration the gallant work she has been doing at Lamorbey Park, Sidcup. In the prefatory poem written for this book, the Poet Laureate recollects in tranquillity one of his visits to the extremely active training college of Speech and Drama which bears Miss Bruford's name. She has been able to work out a strenuous but well balanced dual course, covering in three years not only a whole range of specialized techniques in speech, mime, acting, production and all aspects of stage work, but also concurrently with this, a well devised scheme of training in class-teaching, comprising educational theory and organization, child development and teaching methods, together with extensive supervised teaching practice in Kent schools. At least half of the thirty or forty students who annually complete their three-year course of training take up full-time teaching posts, some in independent schools, but the majority in secondary and primary schools under Local Authorities. A dozen or more of them are now, to my knowledge, doing valuable work as qualified teachers in the county of Kent.

They have had a thorough, even a gruelling training, fitting them to meet with alacrity some of the recently increased interest in the oral side of English work in schools—in speech training, in spoken verse and prose and in dramatic adventures in classrooms and in school halls.

The basis of this specialist training, in Miss Bruford's view, lies in the thorough teaching of mime; and the potential scope of work in this field, as expounded in challenging detail in her book, will come as a revelation to many teachers. For all children the proper conduct of mime work, at a high standard, can be a source of joy and a lighting up of the imagination; and for some—as Miss Bruford shows—mime can have a therapeutic value, as a spur for retarded or handicapped children or as a lantern for those who have wandered into miry ways. This expert book should help in the good work.

A. E. DEAN, 1958

Lines for Miss Rose Bruford's Handbook

This is the text-book that the scholars used,
The grammar, lists of words and exercises,
Pondered till struggle into order fused
And skill annulled suspenses with surprises;
These are the clues to joy in many guises
By which the happy learners won the power
To give the saddest heart a jolly hour.

I, who enjoyed the hour, offer praise
To this most patient but rewarding scheme,
By which delight is lured to human ways
Displaying other truth than what may seem,
Bringing the watcher to the land of dream,
Where Wisdom is, and Beauty, with her light,
Blesses, and makes the instant infinite.

This is the text-book: I have seen its fruit,
(Its first fruits) in the England now beginning.
The seed has taken soil and spreaded roots
While England's future still is in the spinning;
What Glory waits, what Laurel for the winning,
Are Youth's to win, as Youth imagine may,
When Hope and ceaseless effort show the way.

To all the unknown scholars who will learn
From these same chapters, let me wish the power
To tread the stony track and not to turn
Until the weariest heart possess its hour.
The barren stock, so long a mock, will flower,
Therefore, endure, for Conquest will ensue,
And England's Spirit waits on what you do.

Therefore, endure, like the heroic those
Who made our England Merry in the past,
Who made Her Symbol once a single Rose,
Though themselves starved in many a bitter blast.
However grim the way, be not aghast,
Endure, for darkness dies, the clouds disperse,
Beyond are Light and all the Universe.

JOHN MASEFIELD, 1958

I

THE NATURE OF MIME

Some of this book will deal with Mime as a useful and happy part of the education of children, especially of shy and backward children; another section will deal with it as a necessary part of training for the life of the theatre, in all its many forms.

Whichever aspect of it is our concern, certain fundamentals obtain. Teacher or performer needs not only to be physically prepared but also to be himself creative.

In training children a teacher should seek, with great care, what difficulties hinder and what exercises may reveal and encourage the talent that may be made manifest in the awakened and helped nature.

All the exercises mentioned here are designed to help such discovery. They should not be used, and cannot be helpfully used, without understanding of the purpose for which they have been imagined.

The teacher will have to use his imagination not only in thinking of new examples for mime, but also in such a way that the normal life of the individual is borne in mind and not overlooked. Usually the child of poverty will find great joy in miming richness and plenty, and so for a time experiencing this feeling by:

Being a King or a Princess
Receiving rich presents
Wishing, and the wishes coming true.

The more sheltered child of rich parents finds these suggestions dull, and would respond more readily to:

Being a beggar or a tramp
Peeling potatoes and shelling peas
Opening a cupboard and finding everything stolen.

The example must be within the range of the child's knowledge or imagination, and yet not uncomfortably near to circumstances which are in themselves hard for him to bear. This was acutely noticeable when teaching at a Borstal Institution, where girls were allowed to attend classes as a reward for good behaviour over a certain period; they were not allowed to have any books, not even a pencil and paper, so a mime class was exactly the right medium for them; but if an exercise or example touched their own lives too closely, it was met with lethargy and black looks, while if asked to act a film-star or a successful professional woman, instead of being on the defensive, they would use all their energies to give a sincere performance.

The work could then be used as a power in the right direction, not just an outlet into a world of fantasy. Ultimately they achieved some scenes of real beauty, largely concerned with nature; through these they became prepared in mind to listen to great poetry. Their appreciation of the classics was instantaneous, though the majority had never read a poem before.

In working with mentally retarded children, examples also need careful selection. Much patience is needed. It may be necessary to sit quietly with a child for a long time. Perhaps he may play with you at sitting by a fire, or at being in the

ntil at last he will have faith in your
e will enjoy and copy and in the end

been entirely unco-operative for two
een to be moving her hands and arms
urning a handle, and asked what she was
said "I sewing". These were her first
, and marked the beginning of her general

schools the selection of examples can be
eral and cover a wider range, and it will be
at good mime training gives poise and an ease in
nship, especially in adolescence when mime can serve
legitimate outlet for a pent-up and growing emotional
feeling.

The exercises in this book are not meant as systems for the entertainment of school-children, but as a means to a greater grace of life, or to skill in a complex and difficult profession.

Development from mime to utterance of sounds and from these to improvised speech and acting is clearly of value in the development of the whole personality or *person* of either child or adult. Activity is natural. Life is movement. A baby points or reaches to get what it wants; failing in this it utters cries and continues the movement: after this, speech follows. Primitive man's pain or pleasure was probably demonstrated by movement and gesticulation, quickly followed by sounds which were the beginning of speech. There is no doubt that expressive movement is spontaneous and natural; this is immediately apparent in watching animals or children. This is the basis from which we must build.

Watch a child—maybe he is waggling his coat to and fro —and telling you he is a goose flapping his wings; unless

we can see it as such, this is not yet mime, but only
tive play. Children have infinite ideas, but only o
expression, and often very little power to sustain.
discipline, freedom, and relaxation can be learnt
quietness and stillness, which are such essential
acting, as well as of life.

Consider scenes like: "Little Miss Muffet" and "Br
the Spider". In both there are moments of dramatic ac
and moments of absolute quiet; but the quietnes
children will tend to neglect.

The same applies in group work; the rowdiest cow
can be encouraged to appreciate that absolute quiet
stillness is of first importance while they are waiting
ambush.

Or interest may be roused in Trappist monks who go
about their work without a word; to act this requires clarity
of thought, control, and discipline.

Working together in a group improves social relationships
and gives a great power of understanding as well as a chance
to consider other people and to co-operate with them. Each
individual in the group will consider what it feels like to be
someone altogether different and will experience the feeling
of, and the reason for, other people's reactions.

I believe that a teacher will find it helpful to begin any
classwork, either with children or with young people, by
giving them exercises that will make them feel at ease. To
give them this sense of freedom, nothing can be surer than
an exercise of noise and lively movement:

Let little children imagine themselves to be dogs barking
at each other, or at being chained up.

A moment later, let them imagine themselves to be the
same dogs suddenly released to be petted, fed or taken
for a walk.

Let the older class imagine themselves to be savages dancing and yelling to bring the rain.

A moment later, let them imagine that the rain has come, the heat gone: they are cool and happy, their thirst quenched and they are gathering their food for supper.

These are very simple exercises, and need not last more than a few minutes, but they will give to both young classes a feeling of restraint removed, and of happiness restored.

This mood is a precious mood in which both classes can and will profit from what follows.

II

STAGE FALLS

I t is helpful to teach stage falls very early in any senior school or young adult course. Little children fall about easily and for fun without hurting themselves. Older children and adults naturally have not the same confidence; an element of fear has crept in, and to fall needs more and more courage as age increases. When, however, the technique is mastered—and after some practice the fall that appeared to be so difficult is really very simple—the achievement and mastery of it give a great feeling of confidence. Once you can safely throw yourself in any direction with abandon no sense of restriction remains.

It is often a help to start with exercises:

> e.g. Droop the head and shoulders.
> Lift the head and shoulders.

Repeat these several times, gradually increasing the movements through the whole body and out to the extremities.

Probably some will droop nearly to the floor, or even sink down to a kneeling or sitting position; and reach up with the arms on the lifting movement.

> Then—Begin again and this time let sound grow, as the movement increases.

With suitable encouragement from the teacher, even a shy adult will respond, so long as the whole class are working together without onlookers. There may be groans of despair on the downward movement, and shouts of joy on the upward one.

Gradually movement and sound will grow more wild and frenzied and the feeling of freedom from restraint is gained, and from this moment the class progresses more easily and happily.

Even with a class of older men and women, this same feeling can be reached through emotional expression in sound, though the movement must of necessity be less. For them falls would be neither suitable nor advisable.

These simple exercises give the teacher the opportunity to begin to make the class aware of the difference between tension and relaxation: a greater consciousness of the full meaning of relaxation must of course be gained later.

Now the stage fall can be attempted, but it is important to have patience and avoid trying to do too much at once. Here follows a description of the process which should cover some weeks of work:

Technical Falls

In principle all falls are the same. The procedure is to kneel, to sit and to lie.

SIDE FALL

If falling to the right, kneel on the right knee, sit over it to the right, swing the arms in a sweeping movement from left to right brushing the floor all the way, and simultaneously lie to the right, with the arms extended to the right, dropping the head so that it is supported on the right arm. At the finish, the body will be outstretched to the right in a long line, arms extended, left leg extended, right knee bent and tucked under left leg.

It is important that the hands and arms sweep round silently to their destination and do not flop to the ground from above, which is noisy.

If the legs are not relaxed they will be inclined to kick up, which they should not do.

If falling to the left the instructions are reversed—kneel on the left knee, sit to the left, lie to the left, arms move from right to left.

BACK FALL

Kneel backwards allowing the foot to cross the line of the body, so that there is room to sit backwards over the kneeling leg (without sitting on the foot); sit backwards; then lie backwards allowing the arms to sweep along the ground on either side until they are nearly overhead. Again it is important that they brush the ground, rather than flop noisily. One knee is bent and tucked under the other leg at the completion of the fall. This should be practised, using either leg for the kneel.

FRONT FALL

Kneel forward on the right knee (keeping the weight on the left leg until the last moment, to avoid bumping forward on the knee). Bring the seat round to the right, and sit as far forward as possible. Sweep the arms round from left until they are extended forwards; lie forwards letting the head drop on the extended arms. Again the hands and arms brush the ground, rather than dropping from above. As before, this should be practised using either leg for the kneel, the directions being adapted accordingly.

In all these falls it is essential to practise slowly and accurately. The temptation to hurry will lead to leaving out either the kneeling or sitting stage, and the fall will never be easy. By degrees speed up, and relax more and more, so that the fall seems like one movement. The aim should be to fall almost silently, like a leaf rustling to the ground. When the technique is understood, the secret of a silent fall is to breathe in and lift on to the toes, also to lift the arms upwards *before* falling. It is almost a drift upwards, giving an impetus to the fall; a preparation for it—rather like a breath before speaking, or a preliminary movement before a tennis stroke. The fall and breathing out must follow the lift without pause.

COLLAPSING FALL

Do not try this until after the others have been thoroughly practised, otherwise it becomes a temptation to use the collapse for every type of fall, and the basic technique is never really mastered. Once relaxation has been fully grasped and practised, the collapsing fall is comparatively easy, but it is essential to have experience in relaxation to be successful with this fall.

Allow the head to droop, the shoulders to droop, and the knees to sag until they are nearly in a kneeling position; in fact, loosen every muscle until real relaxation is achieved, which means that everything crumples, and you gently fall to the ground in a heap, completely relaxed. In this fall the impetus of the drift upwards as used in the other falls would not be of any help. It is possible to vary falls for all purposes, and ultimately no kind of fall should present difficulty.

Dramatic Falls

The basic technique for stage falls given above, must be mastered before there is any attempt to do a fall with dramatic intention. Eventually, as with all other aspects of mime, having a reason for the movement makes it more convincing, as well as being easier to do.

e.g.   Right Fall as if jostled in a crowd.

Left Fall during a boxing match.

Forward Fall (using right leg to kneel) after having tripped.

Forward Fall (using left leg to kneel) after having been shot.

Backward Fall (using right leg to kneel) after a punch on the jaw.

Backward Fall (using left leg to kneel) trying to recoil from someone who is attacking.

Collapsing Fall as if fainting.

Any fall you like conveying that you have taken poison. Finish by rolling over on the ground as if you are in agony.

The drift upwards would now seem out of place and unnatural. In most cases, however, the same impetus of the lift can be used, but used dramatically, e.g. a spasm of pain, which would cause a moment of tension before relaxing into the fall.

III

EXPRESSIVE EXERCISE

The body will be physically expressive only if it is able to be immediately responsive to any demand. This cannot be so unless it is well trained, well poised, and in tune.

Some good movement training is an essential part of good mime, but whatever the technique it must become habitual, so that in expressive work the technique is unconsciously used without having to be consciously considered. The type of exercise used will depend to some extent on the age of the class, the reason for the class, and the kind of children or students in the class.

Broadly speaking it would be safe to say that the younger child is so supple that exercises are seldom necessary. Rhythmical movements with some imaginative significance will do all that is needed in the way of bodily preparation.

Examples of Imaginative Physical Practice for Young Children

Mime skipping
Be a kangaroo
Be a frog in a marsh   These give a variety
Walk like a tortoise   of movements for feet
Walk like a cat   and legs
Be a Jack-in-the-box in action

Show the neck and head of a giraffe
Show an ostrich looking about, and
   then hiding his head in the sand
Be a puppet on strings
Show a bird pecking for crumbs
Show a fledgeling in a nest putting
   up its beak for food
Be a Chinese Mandarin ornament
   with a nodding head

These are largely for head movement, but the whole physique can be employed as well

Be a rubber toy—flabby at first—
   someone blows air into you—you
   are nearly bursting—then the
   cork is removed and you collapse
Be a worm
Be a seal
Be a brightly burning candle—
   gradually you flicker—and finally
   gutter away
Be a corkscrew
Be a golliwog; you are playing—
   you lose some stuffing—someone mends you again

Mainly movements of the torso giving flexibility and freedom

Play with a ball
Wash some clothes, putting on an
   apron to do so
Wash your face and hands
Do some clay-modelling. Show
   what you are making
Be a butterfly
Be a dragon-fly
Hover like a hawk

Mainly for use of hands and arms

As children grow older they seem to enjoy the security of some basic technique and feel happier if they have it.

Very few exercises would be needed in free mime or ordinary classroom work, as the purpose is not performance. Many teachers will find they can devise the exercises they need for this, and will prefer to do so in order that they may link them with the work being done in physical education. It is, however, important that any exercises given should lead to dramatic movement, so that the expressive work grows naturally from the exercise.

Examples

Appropriate shoulder action (swinging in various directions) might precede the occupational movement of *felling a tree*.
Waist turning might precede the movement of *scything*.
Stretching downwards and upwards of the body might precede the action of *flying a kite*.
Flexibility of the joints and muscles of the foot might be practised before *walking stealthily round a house*.
Rippling movements through the body and arms and hands might be practised before expressing movements *of fire and water*.

For those who know it, Greek dance would provide good basic movement, and so would the best form of modern dance.

For the artist in mime (just as for the ballet dancer) some technique must be learned and practised, or the work will never have 'finish'.[1]

All dramatic movement starts in the centre of the body: this is the seat of the emotions. It is advisable therefore to arrange exercises and expressive practice working from the

[1] For this type of student the exercises listed in Irene Mawer's book *The Art of Mime* are in my opinion the most satisfactory, and should be constantly practised, and linked with expressive work.

torso out to the extremities making a sequence named from the human frame in this order:

1. The torso, the main structure directing.
2. The feet and legs, that give the base.
3. The head and neck, that show the poise.
4. The arms and hands, that work.

Think to yourself what these four can show in mime and imagine how each 'age-group' may exercise and use each one.

Please remember that I only offer suggestions that may help you to invent others, not intending them to be slavishly followed. The teacher of mime needs a constant flow of creative ideas.

Age-groups have been classified as:

Infant
Junior
Senior
Adult

These are used in a broad sense, not rigidly representing the age-groups as recognized in the maintained schools of the country. Always remember that much of the work suggested can be done by any age-group. Some little children have unexpected gifts for mime: age has little to do with aptitude. In one school, I so arranged the classes that each included every age from 8 to 18, mixed together. It worked very well indeed, and the children welcomed the arrangement. Here follows a list of

Examples of Expressive Work

for each of the four body-parts, for all ages. The examples are designed to give a wide range of expression in each division.

INFANTS

Little ones will naturally be unaware which part of the body is being employed and why, but it is well that the teacher should know.

TORSO

Response   Feel hot
Feel cold
Sit in a pool at the sea-side
Play in the sand
Play in a hay-field

Clothes   Put on an imaginary dress—take it off—hang it up, or do what you like with it
Do similar actions with an overall, a jumper, a mackintosh, etc.

Character   Be: A lively puppy
A baby
One of the Three Bears
One of your dolls
A bad goblin that becomes good
A mermaid
A flower-seller
A customer at a super-market—reaching and bending to collect goods.
A dustman

FEET AND LEGS

Response   Walk: On soft sand without shoes
On wet sand without shoes
In pools at the sea without shoes
In puddles with shoes on

On pavement, in the squares with
shoes on
Up steps

Clothes   Put on and take off shoes and socks for different
reasons, describe where you are going, etc.

Character   Be: A naughty elf in a wood
A good fairy
A dragon who hates everyone. (The three
can then work together.)
Little Red Riding Hood setting out
Little Red Riding Hood going through
the wood
Little Red Riding Hood going up to
Granny's door, etc.
Jack and Jill
Jack and the Beanstalk
Other fairy tale or nursery rhyme
characters

HEAD AND NECK

Response   Go to sleep
Wake up in the morning
Eat something nice
Eat something nasty
See a bird's nest in a tree
See a fish in a pool
Look into a wood and go and play with some-
one or something you see there

Clothes   Put on mother's hat
Put on a bathing cap   In each case become
Put on a witch's hat   the owner of the head-
Put on a fairy crown   gear

Character   Be: A bird
                  A goose
                  A prince
                  Punch
                  Judy
                  Cinderella
                  Hansel and Gretel. Find the sugar house
                  and eat it

HANDS AND ARMS

Response   Have cold hands—touch ice
             Have fairy hands—touch gossamer
             Touch a bird
             Put hands in hot water
             Hold a wriggly baby fish

Clothes   Put on woolly gloves
             Put on gloves and find a hole in the finger
             Show the feeling in your hand when the gloves
             are removed
             Put on magic gloves. What do they do?

Occupation   Pick flowers
               Pick and blow a dandelion clock
               Make sand pies
               Draw and crayon a picture
               Play with trains
               Play with any toy

Character   Be: The little match girl
                  A Djinn
                  A cobbler
                  A 'bus conductor
                  A witch making spells

THE WHOLE

Go for an imaginary walk across fields in the country, come to a stream, cross a plank, or stepping stones, paddle across; then come to a wood.

(Let the children continue as they like eventually arriving home again.)

*

Go into the fields and pick flowers and do what you like with them—making daisy-chains—giving them away—taking them home and putting them in water, etc.

*

Go for a day to the sea, get into the train, see the sea, go on to the beach, dig, paddle, have lunch, etc., etc., and finally go home.

*

Be a group of elves who make all sorts of magic shoes, give them to someone and show their magic by the effect they have.

*

This sort of practice can be done individually or in a group. Teachers are sometimes tempted to 'talk down' to the children, which makes the whole idea puerile. By all means use the the question and answer method, but let the voice remain natural and genuine, meeting the children as individuals, exciting their imagination, and adopting their ideas. Working in a community in this way, the children gradually learn to understand themselves better. By degrees simple scenes will develop, which can be mimed very informally, with some children being a group of trees or flowers or whatever background may be needed, so that everyone takes part. At this age there should be no audience, and it should not be regarded as serious acting, but as play.

In the same way stories and songs can be brought to life by the children, but they must be encouraged to develop their own ideas and not on any account to reproduce an imitation of movements made by the teacher, which will be quite meaningless to the child, and serve no useful purpose.

JUNIORS

TORSO

Response   Lie in bracken
A bucket of cold water is thrown over you
Someone is tickling you
You are pulled by a dog on a lead
Walk against a strong wind

Feelings   You are going to a party
You are not able to go after all
See someone crying
Listen to a funny story

Clothes   Imagine you are wearing party clothes
Imagine you are wearing a swim-suit
Imagine you are wearing a leotard and tights

Character   Be: A coalman
A policeman
A typist
A Red Indian   Contrast
A dwarf   downward
A Prince who is changed and upwards
into a frog and then freed movements
again

c

FEET AND LEGS

Response   Kick through fallen leaves, wearing shoes
Step over tree trunks, and walk along a fallen trunk, wearing shoes
Walk on rocks, without shoes
Walk on grass which is full of prickles, without shoes

Feelings   Walk: As if you are away on your holidays
As if you are going to see your grandmother
✗ As if you have been told to go for a walk and don't want to
As if you are going to school
As if you are going shopping

Clothes   Wear: A pair of boots
Dancing shoes
No shoes
Walking shoes
Wellington boots
Bedroom slippers

Character   Be: A giant in seven-league boots
A witch
A tight-rope walker
A highwayman

HEAD AND NECK

Response   Try to see something that is just too high for you
Feel too hot
Bump your head unexpectedly
✗ Find you have sand in your mouth

Feelings   Show: You are very bored—show what it is
                     that is boring you
                     You look mischievous   ⎫ You
                     You are looking very guilty   ⎪ must
                     You are convulsed with laugh- ⎬ know
                     ter   ⎭ why

Clothes   Wear: A mackintosh hat
                    A paper hat from a cracker
                    A cowboy's hat
                    A crown
                    A clown's hat

Eye Focus   Look at: An ant-heap
                      A tall tower
                      A train
                      A worm
                      A ship leaving the quay

Character   Be: An old lady
                  Rumpelstiltskin
                  A dressmaker
                  A naughty child
                  A clown

HANDS AND ARMS

Response   Let dry sand run through your fingers
              Prick your finger
              Handle plasticine
              Show sticky fingers

Feelings   Show sleepy hands
              Show agitated hands
              Show idle hands

Clothes	Put on and take off fur gloves without separated fingers
	Show the difference between your best gloves and your oldest gloves
	Put a bandage on one finger
	Put a plaster on one finger
Occupation	Dig a sand castle
	Sew a seam
	Throw and catch a ball
	Paint a picture
Gestures	Express in any way you like:
	"Look up there"
	"Come here"
	"Go away"
	"I hate you"
Character	Be: A shopkeeper—packing up goods—taking money, etc.
	Peter Pan—trying to sew on his shadow.
	Alice in Wonderland—doing anything you like
	A shepherd—tending his sheep

THE WHOLE

Feel that you are a gas-filled balloon—you are anchored to the ground—suddenly the rope snaps, you sail away and away for miles. While you are gaily sailing along, a bird pecks you—the gas escapes—you collapse and fall to the ground.

*

Hold a wish-bone with a friend—make a wish—as you snap the bone your wish comes true—show what you wished for.

*

You are sitting on the top of a high cliff—at the edge of an immense hole—it is known as the Witch's Cauldron—the sea is coming in at high tide. You have been watching it with fascination, and now it is time to go home. Just as you are leaving you see an extra big wave fill the cauldron—it looks as if something is rising in the middle of the whirl-pool—you have a strange feeling about it. Something happens—show what it is.

*

You are sitting by a window—it is summer and it has been a still day, but a gentle wind is beginning to move the trailing honeysuckle at the window. Idly you reach to touch it, but it is wafted away by the wind. Each time you reach, it blows further away, as if some magic in the wind were carrying it. You are determined to catch it and jump to do so—as it breaks off in your hand—something un-expected happens—show what it is.

*

Now let the teacher divide the class into four groups. Each group can be responsible for one of the four seasons, and decide for themselves how to show them—e.g. plant-life, bird-life, farm-life, reaction of humans to the elements, etc.

There can be infinite variety in this exercise and room for development into a play.

SENIORS

TORSO

Sensation   Enjoy the wind on your body
Enjoy the sun on your body
Lie under a tree—a caterpillar falls on you

Be nearly asleep—you are worried by a wasp
Go into a very cold sea
Writhe in agony

Emotion　　Show: Disappointment (failing an exam)
　　　　　　　　　　Delight (going abroad for the first time)
　　　　　　　　　　Fear (sleeping in a haunted room)
　　　　　　　　　　Envy (someone else's success)

(The suggested reasons are to ensure that emotions are not superficially imposed without reason. It is all too easy to do this, which leads to posing and falsity of expression.)

Show: Joy
　　　　Sorrow
　　　　Sympathy
　　　　Amusement, etc

(Let the reason first be thought of by the individual)

Costume　　Wear: A dance dress
　　　　　　　　　A sun-suit
　　　　　　　　　A winter coat
　　　　　　　　　A pair of shorts
　　　　　　　　　A tennis dress

Character　　Be: A sailor
　　　　　　　　A hunchback
　　　　　　　　A ring-master of a circus
　　　　　　　　A savage

FEET AND LEGS

Sensation　　Walk: On heather wearing shoes
　　　　　　　　　　On mud wearing suitable shoes
　　　　　　　　　　On mud wearing unsuitable shoes
　　　　　　　　　　On pebbles without shoes
　　　　　　　　　　On springy turf without shoes
　　　　　　　　　　Through a mountain stream

Emotion	Show: Pleasure Hesitation Determination Stealth	(Again it is important that the reason for the feeling is thought out by the individual or it will never ring true)

Costume Wear: Shoes that are too large
Shoes that are too small
Skates
Fisherman's boots

Character Be: An athlete
A burglar
An Eastern man or woman
A 'bus conductor on his 'bus

HEAD AND NECK

Sensation Feel water trickling down your neck in the rain
Show your reaction when something hits you on the head
Feel an irritation
Show that you have a headache

Emotion Show: Shyness
Curiosity
Certainty
Enjoyment
}(Develop reasons why)

Costume Wear: A smart hat
A sou'wester
A bathing cap
Tie a scarf round your head

Eye-Focus Look at the stars
Look at the horizon
Look at a picture

Look in a shop window
Watch a jet aeroplane
Watch sea breaking under a cliff
Search in the sand for something you have lost

Character   Be: A Spanish lady
A Hockey International
An artist
A prim lady of 65
A gipsy

HANDS AND ARMS

Sensation   Trail your hand in the water from a boat
Mistakenly put your hand in a pot of jam
Mix flour
Pick roses with many thorns

Emotion   Show: Angry hands
Frightened hands
Imperious hands

Costume   Try to put on gloves that are too small
Wear: Gloves that are too long in the fingers
Fur-lined gloves
Silk gloves

Occupation   Show: Knitting
Scrubbing a table
Hammering in a nail
Peeling and eating a banana
Peeling an orange

Gestures   Express in any way you like:
"You dare!"
"No, I won't"
"Please come with me"
"Help! I am lost"

Character Be: A weight-lifter
             A dentist
             A draper's assistant
             A student
             A hairdresser

THE WHOLE

You are in a garden—show that a stream runs through it, that there is a high wall on one side of it, and that you can look across a valley below you to a mountain range. Live in that garden and, as well as showing the scene, convey the atmosphere.

*

Show that you are in a busy street crowded with shoppers; you are anxious to see what is in the shop windows. Show what you see and whether or not it pleases you. Finally, come across something you have been wanting for years—decide whether or not you will buy it—show what it is like.

*

Show that you are walking up a wooded glen following the river—you are surprised to find that it ends in a waterfall which cannot be passed, and which covers you with spray—you take pleasure in watching the salmon leaping to the upper reaches of the river.

*

Show that you are lying on the rocks near a lagoon in the South Pacific—the sun is beating down and you are enjoying relaxing in the water—or in your little boat moored to the rocks nearby—suddenly there is a cry from your companions of "Sharks!"

*

Show the way people move at different periods of their life—try to show what you imagine you felt like when you were just learning to walk and movement was rather perilous and uncertain—then show the same child firmly established in life at the age of seven—again aged fourteen, twenty-one, forty, fifty-five, seventy, ninety; or whatever ages you like to select. (The young will always fall into the trap of making fifty quite decrepit, and have nothing left for what comes after!)

Develop further by thinking of different types of people in each age-group; how do they feel, and therefore how do they move? (The reason for their mode of movement is all-important, otherwise the average student will develop a *facility* in expression which can be entirely superficial, and will never be convincing to any spectator.)

*

You are in a forest in a foreign country. A group of you set out to cross it, not knowing what you may meet. Show your adventures—crossing deep water—avoiding wild creatures—watching birds drinking at a pool—finally you reach habitation, and are glad of shelter. Night falls, your voices are heard round your camp fire, and the distant sounds of the forest die away.

(In this sort of scene some noise would be permissible, and some members of the class might be mainly responsible for it.)

*

A group sets out on a journey—show the excited antici-pation, the catching of the train, the arrival,—then boarding the boat—the movement of the boat,—it pitches and tosses —there is a storm—you are wrecked. Show your adventures after that, and a final safe return.

OR

—the ending of the journey as originally planned and a safe return.

*

(Perhaps only one or two characters may begin a scene but gradually all members of a class will find themselves contributing to it.)

ADULT

TORSO

Sensation   Take a cold shower
Battle with a hailstorm
Lie in hot sun
Lie in gentle rain
Show you are being lashed with whips
Show you are at sea
Be a Spirit in torment (as in Dante's *Inferno*)

Emotion   Show: Despair—having lost your job and having no money
Confidence—having just left College
Anxiety—watching someone who is ill
Ecstasy—you are just engaged to be married

(Repeat all these—thinking of different reasons for the same feeling.)

Costume   Wear: A fur cape
Slacks
A long evening dress
A cloak
A sari
A Roman toga

Character Be: A beggar
A butler
A matron of a hospital
A slave
A drug addict
A street performer

FEET AND LEGS

Sensation Walk over barnacles, without shoes
Walk on hot asphalt, without shoes
Walk in the sea—knee deep
Try to get out of a bog—wearing shoes
Walk in deep snow—wearing shoes
Walk on heather—wearing shoes
Walk over gravel—dressed for a dance
Stand in the Underground after a day's work

Emotion Show: Sadness
Eagerness
Doubt
Jubilance
}(Think of reasons first)

Costume Wear: Heavy boots
Sandals
Sandals with a buckle off
High heels
Sloppy shoes

Character Be: A farmer
A thief
A dancer
A scrubber
A model

HEAD AND NECK

Sensation Show: Giddiness
                   Drunkenness
             Avoid something that is going to hit you
             Carry a heavy basket of fruit on your head

Emotion Show: Sorrow ⎫
                  Freedom ⎪
                  Pride   ⎬ (Develop reasons)
                  Tolerance ⎭

Costume Wear: A modern hat
                 A picture hat
                 A nun's habit
                 A pierrot's conical hat
                 A crash helmet

Eye Focus Watch: Clouds
                    A snail
                    Birds
                    A tennis match
                    A frog jumping
             Look for a book in a bookcase
             Look in a mirror

Character Be: A blind man
                 A jester
                 A general
                 A short-sighted old gentleman
                 Comus
                 A Puritan lady
                 Mephistopheles

HANDS AND ARMS

Sensation Touch fur
             Touch muslin

Touch satin
Handle wood
Feel and find a secret panel in the drawer of
an old desk
Cut your finger
Put your hand on a jelly-fish
Receive an electric shock

Emotion   Show: Terror
              Menace   (Show your reasons for
              Gentleness   them)
              Exultation

Costume   Wear: Mittens
              Tight kid gloves
              Surgical gloves
              Gardening gloves
              Long gloves

Occupation   Saw wood
              Fish, in a river
              Prepare and cook potatoes
              Use a sewing machine
              Write a letter
              Go shrimping

Gestures   Express in any way you like:
              "Bring that here"
              "You naughty dog"
              "I love you"
              "Look, thirty elephants are coming down
              the road"
              "I dress beautifully when I am going to
              play the fiddle"

Character   Be: A sculptor
                    A household help
                    A lady of leisure
                    A porter
                    A bar attendant
                    A musician
                    An actress
                    A tramp

THE WHOLE

You are sitting in a cell in solitary confinement; you have been there for a very long time and are accustomed to silence—your mood is of despair. You hear a distant knocking—tension and excitement grow in you as you listen—it fades—you decide it was only a figment of your imagination.

*

Repeat the same scene—but the knocking is real—it is a signal which has to be passed on from cell to cell—you have been waiting for it—eagerly you join in the knocking and pass on the message.

*

Repeat the scene again—but this time the sound brings escape—you stagger out into the open dazed by the light and by the sight of the world beyond—react to it.

*

You are sight-seeing, visiting a beautiful castle—you look at all the antiques, pictures, suits of armour, etc.—then you come into a room full of mirrors and catch sight of yourself—you alter your posture and way of walking, again you catch a glimpse of yourself on the other side of the room,

and find again that you do not walk as you thought you did!
You forget yourself, and return to the magnificence of
the room you are in.

*

Repeat this scene as someone else, who has different
reactions from yours, and will therefore respond differently.

*

You are a fisherwoman gathering sea-weed on the shore,
it is a sunny day, life around you is active, boats are putting
out, the older men are mending the nets—you say good-bye
to the men-folk who go out for their day's fishing.

*

You are the same woman but on a very different day. The
sky is overcast and high seas are running. You are working
in your house, but anxiety takes you out to the cliff-top to
look for the boats. End the scene as you like.

*

Sometimes it will be noticeable that a performance is
unconvincing, but the reason may not be apparent. It will
then be useful to the teacher to be able to analyse the expressive power of each part of the body. He may well find that
although the mood is expressed in face or body, the feet
and legs are not in keeping with the rest. This frequently
happens with beginners. Each individual will of course
have his own particular weakness, but the power of the
various parts having been established, they must finally be
blended into a harmonious whole.

Consider for a moment the power of the hands alone.

Say to the class:
Put your hands out in front of you and look at them. The

use of your hands is very revealing and shows quite a lot about you. Imagine they are going to be photographed, and consider if you looked at such a photograph whether you would recognize the person to whom they belong. Hold them again in front of you. Without rushing, change from one feeling to another:

Examples

Juniors	*Seniors*	*Adults*
Strong hands	Greedy hands	Avaricious hands
Gentle hands	Kind hands	Be-ringed hands
Fierce hands	Cruel hands	Sorrowful hands
Flabby hands	Useless hands	Luxury-loving hands
Magic hands	Useful hands	Uncertain hands
Nervous hands	Angry hands	Artistic hands
Pleading hands	Frightened hands	Determined hands

(Do not trouble infants with such detailed work as this.)

*

When these expressions have been established in the hands, it is a useful practice gradually to add the other parts of the body, and ultimately from the feeling aroused, to build a whole character.

Example

Greedy Hands—add a greedy face, and the sort of body that goes with it—feel it in arms, neck, and shoulders; now add the legs and feet, and begin to move about—Do an occupation—Show where you are, and where you are going —whether anyone is with you, and whether or not you are happy—if not, what is your mood and intention?

Gradually in this way, the character will grow to be someone you can believe in, provided you fill out all the real thoughts and feelings of the person, and don't leave only a

D

shell that is simply an outward appearance, with no motive force of spirit.

Having practised this, you will find that any of the examples listed for hands could equally well be used for feet, body, head, etc. Try some of them starting with another part, and gradually add the rest, perhaps bringing the hands in last.

All this will increase your awareness of the capacity of each separate part of your body and remind you that ultimately you must be a *whole*.

*

All the examples listed in this chapter are carefully selected so that there is scope for the particular part that is being practised. It is advisable to remind yourself of the heading all the time you are practising, so that the best use is made of the particular examples. Otherwise it is all too easy to treat *all* examples as free expression, forgetting the need to find your ability with each part first.

It is quite a good plan at frequent intervals to revert to a natural walk round the room without any thought of characterization. The practice and analysis will have given some freedom, new confidence, and poise.

Exercises—like vain repetition of prayer—will not in themselves be any use. It is the way they are done that matters. They need great concentration always, and there should be some improvement and greater freedom and finish each time they are performed. As with other Arts—ninety per cent of the students seem to think that running through the practice at great speed will have a magical effect, and having performed this ritual, they are surprised that their work is no better.

For any art, concentration and regularity of practice are needed; the true artist knows this, and brings all his energy and his being into his work. Only then can there be real results.

There is considerable talent to be found everywhere; there are numbers of people who can arrive at quite good standards by sheer hard work and tenacity of purpose. Alas, only very rarely is there a blend of real gift with complete concentration and persistent hard work. When this is found the result is inspired brilliance.

IV

RELAXATION

It may seem strange that I have not talked much of relaxation until this point, as it is so fundamental a part of all movement.

I have found, however, that classes are more able to grasp the full significance of relaxation and to make use of it, after they have done some spontaneous expressive work. Then they find that, if relaxed, they can do everything much more easily.

Unless there is this incentive, and understanding of the need for relaxation, there is a tendency for the young to turn from it, since activity is so much more natural to them. A simple way to illustrate the necessity for relaxation is to refer back to the stage fall, which will obviously be more effectively performed if it is completely relaxed.

The processes described here cannot all be achieved in one or two lessons; they will cover some weeks of work. The development will often be very slow, but always worth while. Strength of movement grows from relaxation, and in beauty of movement relaxation is always apparent.

The mind governs bodily movement: but if the body is really deeply relaxed, relaxation of mind usually follows. It is not easy for the average person to go through the necessary processes to achieve this state. The harder he

tries the less he can relax; it is contrary to all other learning
to be asked not to try, but instead to allow the muscles to
be at rest, and in fact to loosen the reins of control. Also,
the more he is in need of relaxation, the less he will want
to discipline himself to achieve it, and relaxation does require
self-discipline.

Often, rather than relaxing, people seem to find it easier
to remain in a state of nervous tension and irritability.

In learning to relax, it is necessary first to appreciate the
weight of each limb when it is not moved by muscular
activity.

Lie flat on the back, feeling as if your limbs are heavy as
lead. Let someone lift your hand or arm. The natural
instinct is always to help by lifting it yourself. Avoid this—
leave it as if without life. Then the limb will fall heavily
and limply to the ground, without a moment's hesitation in
the air; (any hesitation would be a sign of tension). Each of
the limbs can be tested in the same way. Sometimes if the
leg is lifted underneath the knee, you will be tempted to raise
the whole leg—this again is a sign of tension. If completely
relaxed, it is possible to lift the knee joint only, leaving the
foot sliding along the ground.

These are merely initial tests as part of the first experience
of letting go.

Now try to stretch as far as possible in every direction,
just as an animal does before lying down by a fire; then let
go; this helps you to release. Choose any set of muscles you
like (e.g. wrist or neck or toe) and tense it for a period. You
will want to release it; continue tensing beyond that point
so that on releasing it you will become aware of the comfort
of relaxation. Then enjoy that feeling of release. Feel consciously that you can enjoy the same looseness in your whole
body.

Take a few slow easy breaths, and each time you breathe

out imagine that all effort oozes from you with the outgoing
breath. Do not be afraid to move if you are uncomfortable;
being uncomfortable will itself cause tenseness. Be as easy
as you can, but remain on your back with your hands at your
sides, not overhead. You will find in time that you can
succeed equally well whether you are on a soft bed or a
hard floor. Send a thought to each part of your body in
turn. As you think of each part remember that you must not
try to *do* anything—simply ask yourself "Is it relaxed?" It is
quite a laborious process, and much easier to achieve if an
outsider suggests the thought for you. If such assistance is
available, the suggestions must be given sufficiently slowly
and without any suggestion of hypnosis, though a calm quiet
voice will obviously be a help to the realization of what is
required.

When you have sent a thought to each part, return to any
that may have proved to be too tense—perhaps the hollow
of your back, the nape of your neck, the jaw and tongue,
behind the eyes, and so on. Just let them sink, and imagine
yourself to be floating away into a state of happy uncon-
sciousness. Feel the blood flowing easily through your
veins, and imagine sunlight pouring through them. Any
images that help to give the feeling are valuable. If your
mind is still centred on a conversation you will find that
your speech muscles will not be relaxed; and similarly if
you are seeing something vividly with your mind, your eye
muscles will be too lively. Let go, and enjoy the lack of
responsibility—and *rest*.

Even then you may need to anchor your mind if it is to be
at rest. Choose a tranquil scene—a blue sky, a still lake, or
a peaceful colour such as green. Some people prefer to think
of black and find it excludes all else: others like to imagine
they are lying still, almost floating, while nature moves
round them. It is impossible to think of nothing, but it is not

impossible to concentrate on one of these ideas. Choose the one that suits you best, and do not waver. Gradually and with constant practice, relaxation will come, but it needs concentration in the initial stages.

After deep relaxation of this kind, it is very unwise to jump up quickly, or rush back into activity, you may experience giddiness if you do. Sit up slowly, and stay sitting for a few minutes. Breathe and stretch, then stand and walk round easily, feeling that you are using the muscles that are necessary, and no others. Do not be distressed if you are sleepy, this will mean you have succeeded. By degrees your result will be achieved more and more quickly and after some practice, physical relaxation should be possible instantly—as is necessary in the stage fall.

Classes gain enormously from this ability to relax. The most undisciplined are often those who need and enjoy it most—and if they go to sleep do not worry, but be glad. The very fact that they do so proves that they have relaxed successfully.

During the war, working with groups of boys and girls in their late teens and in a place where discipline was unknown, and chaos and noise were perpetual, I found the only way of achieving any serious work in mime was by starting each class with relaxation. This was soon accepted as a natural situation, and it worked miracles. Late-comers (inevitable in those uncertain days) instead of entering noisily would creep in on tiptoe and lie down with the others. The result was that twice the amount of work was accomplished in half the time, and it was done with zest and interest, instead of the time being frittered away and treated as an opportunity to add to the general tumult.

In all movement or drama classes, discipline can be difficult, for sheer enthusiasm can create turbulence. Moments of quiet are essential, and as all the civilized world seems to need to learn to relax the practice can be beneficial from every point of view, apart from the fact that for good movement it is an essential basis.

Having developed the habit of relaxation[1] so that you can use it at will, it is necessary to appreciate that during all action some groups of muscles are relaxed while other opposing muscles are tensed; also that most people use far too much effort to carry out simple everyday actions—e.g. dressing, washing, and so on. This excess of effort is very noticeable if your hand slips while doing one of these actions and hits a piece of furniture! The impact is unexpectedly great, and you will usually find that you could have achieved the desired result with half the effort.

Movement will benefit from relaxation, and become altogether more free; naturally it must not be slovenly, but easy and well poised.

The word relaxation is commonly used, but it is still uncommon to find a real understanding of its meaning.

[1] Anyone who is sufficiently interested to wish to study the subject more deeply should read *Relaxation* by Maurice Jacobson.

V

OCCUPATIONAL WORK

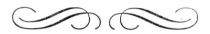

Occupational work takes our minds back into the past and forward into the future. It covers any and every daily action and belongs to all generations of mankind. In itself an occupational action is not of particular interest. The reason for it, the surroundings, the people who make the action, their feelings—these immediately hold the elements of drama. This should be in our minds when we teach occupational action in mime.

So many classes seem to work away at realistic details which can be of no interest to anyone. When we paint a field we do not set down every blade of grass, we give an impression in which those who view the picture can believe. In miming an occupation we give an impression of an action which is accepted as truth by the onlookers although the mime may actually take much less time than the real action. Occupational mime has many practical uses. Children seated in desks, or working in a small space, can enjoy this work when other branches of mime might not be possible. With young children it is especially valuable and stimulates and disciplines their natural inventive powers and imagination.

With older children in their school plays, as indeed with all serious adult actors, there is obvious benefit. How seldom are the stage properties available before the last few rehearsals! How often one sees the timing of a scene, which has been carefully planned beforehand, completely upset, because an occupational action, such as pouring out tea, was not properly anticipated—the actor's mime having been inadequate!

Children are apt to attempt too much at once, which usually gives a blurred result. They should be encouraged to think on simple lines at first, and to make one action recognizable at a time.

A group of boys will decide to be highwaymen, riding, lassoing, sniping, stealing; they will make none of these actions clear, but merge them all into one, in their excitement about their story. They will, however, enjoy themselves very much more when they have given time to direct their imagination into the particular channel that is required. Let them express their feelings, and all that they personally want to express, but let them understand that they must be selective, and concentrate on the sequence of events, one at a time, and as if they were all true.

Here are some suggestions for practice:

Let the class begin by shutting their eyes, excluding everyone and everything about them. Then in their minds, without movement, go through the simple action of undoing a button. Then—quite slowly—again only in their minds, let them do it up again.

Now ask them to make the movements they have imagined, and they will find the doing strangely real, because the imagination has been used.

Treat another simple action in the same way, as for example, mentally tying up a bow or taking off a sweater. After they have done the action very carefully in the mind only, let them attempt to mime it perfectly.

This amount of concentration and absorption is needed in all mime, especially in showing an occupation.

Now try to develop a sense of weight and size.

Describe the size of an object to the class and ask them to imagine they are holding it. They must feel the weight of it, then be conscious of the shape of it, touch it as if they were holding it, look at it, think about it, come to know it and to establish a proprietary interest in it.

Try this with the following objects

Infants	*Juniors*
A ball of wool	A snowball
A big book	A glass tumbler
A silkworm	Two cherries on a stalk
A spoon	A sack of coal
A kitten	A bunch of flowers
An egg	A bucket and spade

Seniors	*Adults*
A pile of books	A cake
A garden rake	An electric iron
A paper weight	A cigarette
A puppy	A basket of potatoes
A cricket ball	A horse-shoe
A mail bag	The week-end shopping

Then having experienced the weight, shape, and feeling of the different objects, let them each fetch one (still in mime) from a suitable spot, give it to someone else, and let him put it down. Let them get used to handling and exchanging these objects. The children's success will be gained by their own belief in what they are doing.

Now pass on to other objects which are of such a nature that action is indicated. If the articles are of a sort that can be opened, let them do so and show what is inside; ask them in each case to *use* the object in any way that seems suitable.

Examples

Infants	Juniors
A handbag	A parcel
A bag of sweets	A work box
An umbrella	A garden hose
A box of bricks	A bottle of ink

Seniors	Adults
A wooden box	A suitcase
A bucket of water	A coal scuttle
A change of clothing	A pair of skis
A candle	A mower

It is sometimes a good plan to divide classes into halves, and allow one half to watch the other half, taking it in turns: or to divide into couples, so that each person has his own partner, and one can watch the other, and say what is clear and what cannot be understood.

Then it is useful to analyse which part of the arm is mainly used for certain actions. Although it is true that more often than not all the muscles are used in some degree, yet the concentration of the movement may be in a particular part, as in these examples, which are worth trying:

FINGERS AND HANDS

Infants	Juniors
Threading beads	Writing
Playing with toy soldiers	Winding a watch
Making a daisy chain	Plaiting

Seniors	Adults
Sewing	Painting a miniature
Playing cards	Examining jewels
Counting coins	Shelling peas

WRISTS

Infants
Turning on a tap
Playing with sand
Stirring a mug of cocoa

Juniors
Using an indiarubber
Hammering with a small hammer
Cutting out a paper picture

Seniors
Sharpening a pencil
Winding a small clock
Using a pair of compasses

Adults
Pinning up a hem on the wearer
Typing
Using a small screwdriver

ELBOWS

Infants
Ringing a bell
Weighing and putting sweets in a bag
Spinning a humming top

Juniors
Bouncing a ball
Beating a gong
Playing draughts

Seniors
Polishing shoes
Turning the handle of a sewing machine
Arranging large flowers in a vase

Adults
Wringing out a wet sheet
Winding a large ball of wool
Jacking up a car

SHOULDERS

Infants
Making a 'snowman'
Digging
Beating time with music

Juniors
Stirring a Christmas pudding
Pumping a bicycle tyre
Pulling a sledge

Seniors	*Adults*
Polishing a floor	Hanging washing on a line
Playing tennis	Pushing a car
Using a pick	Hauling a sail

Once again the classes will no doubt supply other ideas and there may be plenty of argument about the way in which all these things are done. All this is healthy, and the argument can only end in whether or not the general effect is one in which an onlooker can believe.

Some accurate practice in varying occupations should then follow. Take the simple example of *using a hammer*. *Try to knock a nail into a wall*. Nine out of ten people will hold the hammer normally in their right hand and the nail in their left, and will then make the mistake of letting the right fist contact the nail, not judging accurately the length of the hammer or allowing for the head of the hammer to reach the nail—which means the right hand should be well below the left. This sounds so elementary when it is written, but the mistake is a constant one! Similarly, ask someone to mime *scrubbing the floor*. The main action will often be realistic, but frequently the hand will be found to be clenched so that it could not be holding a brush, the imaginary brush being on the floor with no allowance for the length of the bristles! In the simple action of *sewing*, everyone will push the needle into the material, but the majority will then make a continuous movement instead of releasing the fingers to take up the point to pull it out! Asked to *handle a bucket of water*, nearly always the distance from the ground will vary each time it is put down, the action of the handle will be exaggerated, and the difference in weight when it is full or empty will not be clearly shown.

In the case of small articles, as for instance reels of cotton, they will start one size, but will shrink and expand in use!

When illustrating these points to a class examples could be quoted indefinitely, but the teacher must beware of spending too much time on detail and so making the class dull. It is sufficient that the difficulties be grasped in such a way that the principle of the work is established. Interest in the work will automatically follow.

The next stage then is to consider who is doing the action and why. Much the best way is to gather ideas from those who are carrying out the occupations, but, by way of illustration, I will indicate below the sort of suggestions which might apply, basing them on some of the earlier examples.

INFANTS

Ringing a bell as:
> Mother letting you know it is dinner-time
> A man ringing a doorbell
> Teacher ringing the school bell

Turning on a tap as:
> A gardener who is going to fill a watering can
> A naughty child letting it run for fun
> A woman at the kitchen sink

JUNIORS

Playing draughts as:
> Someone who is learning the game
> A small boy who hates playing
> A very earnest old gentleman who has played all his life

Stirring a Christmas pudding as:
> Father of the family, just home from work
> The cook who is making it
> A visitor who has just called

SENIORS

Using a pair of compasses as:
>A lethargic schoolgirl doing her homework
>A neat, very short-sighted little boy
>A clever architect

Polishing a floor as:
>A very fat elderly lady who is very hot
>A child who is full of energy
>A rather affected young man

ADULTS

Typing as:
>A head-mistress whose secretary is away
>A young person who is struggling to do it with one finger
>A very efficient secretary.

Pinning up a hem on the wearer as:
>Mother, having made the child's dress
>Younger sister, trying to satisfy an older sister who is going to a dance
>An old dressmaker, who is well accustomed to it.

As character is added in this way, the pupils will immediately begin to show more individuality and vitality, and enjoyment will grow; the difficulty often arises that in their excitement about the character, the occupation becomes vague and indeterminate and a reminder is necessary.

A good deal of work can be done on these lines which will lead naturally into scenes using occupational movement. Before developing these it is well to appreciate that in a play all characters are expressing some sort of feeling. At any moment in life, any person, or a group of people, may be doing ordinary everyday actions—washing up, digging the garden, smoking a pipe, eating lunch, and so on, but at *all* times these actions are accompanied by some emotion, however slight. The mind is not always occupied with the action, but may be centred on some other more absorbing interest, which means—in acting—that the occupation is being done, by a particular character and with a particular feeling or emotion which may or may not be related to the occupational action. In a play or a scene so much happens in a short space of time that the emotion is a very important part of the situation, and usually the occupation alone would seem dull. Therefore the occupational action must appear to be so natural that the emotion of the imagined situation holds the audience. With or without stage properties, this naturalness requires a good deal of practice.

A further good exercise, therefore, is to use the foregoing examples of occupation and character adding emotion to them, making quite sure that occupation and character are not lost when emotion is added.

For example

SENIORS

Using a pair of compasses as the three characters already given. Act all three first expressing the emotion of *despair*, and then all three expressing the emotion of *hope*. Similarly *polishing the floor* as the three characters already given first expressing the emotion of *sorrow*, and then all three again expressing the emotion of *happiness*.

Be watchful to see that these emotions are not put on artificially. The test for this is to question the class individually to find out what reason was behind the expression of that emotion.

E

Many reasons may be given; one might expect, for example, that the *lethargic schoolgirl* might easily be in *despair* about her work, on the other hand her lethargy might well be caused because she had been to a dance the night before and was daydreaming of the boy-friend; her expression of *hope* could equally easily spring from either. The *short-sighted boy* might be in *despair* because he had failed his examination which would affect his future career, or the emotion might be quite unconnected with his work,—perhaps because his dog had been run over. Equally *hope* could spring from the opposite of either of these thoughts. The *clever architect* might be doing his job perfectly, but the emotion of *despair* could be caused by his wife's serious illness, and equally the emotion of *hope* by her recovery.

In the same way the *fat elderly lady,* the *energetic child* and the *affected young man* would most likely be suffering *sorrow* about something quite unrelated to the polishing of the floor, but their work would probably be slower as a result; the feeling of *happiness* would bring activity to whatever they were doing, and perhaps a song or a whistle!

ADULTS

Typing as the three characters already given. Act all three, first expressing the emotion of *doubt*, and then all three expressing the emotion of *confidence*.

Similarly—*pinning up a hem* as all three characters already given. Act all three, first expressing the emotion of *fear*, and then of *relief*.

Again it will be advisable to ensure that the emotions have been real by questioning, and remember that the occupation in question is often quite secondary to the feeling and emotion hidden in the mind. When acting, however, these emotions which in real life are hidden, must be clearly shown in the way that that particular character would show them. It is not easy to keep occupations, character, and emotion all in unity. An actor in performance must keep to the character he is acting, and if a lady drops her fan or handkerchief, he must pick it up and return it *in character*, at the same time showing his *emotion* towards the lady.

Another point to be remembered in connection with all acting, and with occupational mime in particular, is that it is sometimes necessary to magnify what is being done in order that the audience may be able to follow it.

This does not mean being untrue, it merely involves some slight emphasis in the exhibition of the act being performed, e.g., if miming darning, let it be seen, by putting it in a better light as if it is difficult or dark; this looks and is natural and an audience can understand the reason for it.

Examples for Infants and Juniors have not been listed in this 'emotional' work as it is not really suitable for them, though, of course, there can be no harm in asking them to show whether they are enjoying or disliking what they are doing, or whether the person they are acting is enjoying or disliking it.

Up to this point, my remarks on occupational mime have been kept to hand and arm movements. Try now to show the strains and stresses of the body during work. Try all the suggested movements with the natural reactions of all the body. This can be felt in an action such as *pushing* or *pulling*: the same applies, naturally, in all *lifting* or *winding* movements, and strength of action will be gained by a concentration on the Torso. Feel also that with a big movement like *swinging a roadmender's hammer* or *pulling a heavy rope* the feet and legs and back are very strongly employed; in a lesser degree this also applies to the smaller actions; but always the base must be firm, and the spine is usually active.

Perhaps the reaction of the head to occupational movement may not seem so obvious, but in fact, there are very few actions which do not bring a strong reaction from the head, and a very vital lesson could well be devoted to this subject alone. Think of *knocking in a nail, catching a ball, digging, jacking up a car,* and many other obvious instances. In a lesser degree with even small actions, the reflex action of the head is present.

It is important in mime to know what each part can do separately, but it is equally important to realize that no part works in complete isolation. Movement is rhythm, involving the *whole body*.

This reaction of strain and stress of the whole may be more noticeable in some of the heavier examples. When carrying a *bucket full of water, a very heavy suitcase,* or a *sack of coal,* some muscles are working against others, reacting to the strain. In the actual doing of these things the more muscles that can be relaxed the easier the job will be. In miming the action it is necessary to feel which set of muscles will be tensing, which relaxing. If the mime is good, on finishing the action it will be felt as if it had been real, and the muscles will have worked in that way.

Schoolgirls and boys enjoy miming every kind of sport. To begin with, let them mime the separate actions that may be needed, e.g. throwing and catching balls of varying sizes and textures, handling the tennis racket, cricket bat, hockey stick, etc.—then let each join with a partner and mime passing the ball between them, watching carefully the weight, speed, and power of the pass so that it is suitably received. A good preparation is to divide the class into small circles and to let them mime throwing a ball across and about the circle, noticing carefully when it drops, how it is thrown, and giving a real reaction to it. Ultimately set the whole game as if on a real field. and let them try to play it.

Accuracy, a sense of weight, a response to other people, and a great deal of pleasure will be gained from this practice.

This can lead into a form of team-race, which differs from the normal race in that it will be judged, not by speed, but by accuracy of definition. Set the leader of each team an imaginary object to carry up and down the room—e.g. a rabbit, a bicycle, a vase of flowers, a bottle of wine, etc.— according to the age of the group. The leader having carried it back to his place passes it to the next who carries it up and down and so it passes on through the team. The rest of the team turn their backs until the one before them is performing, which ensures that they must take what they see, without having witnessed the original performance of the leader. The team which finishes with the same object as that with which it started is the winner—and it is not so easy as it sounds! The game can also be played from other angles: instead of using it occupationally it can be used similarly for character work, costume work, or any other aspect of mime.

Another test for a group at work:

Let a group carry any object, such as a piano, an instrument of an orchestra, fire appliances, or a folded tent,—and set it down. Another group recognizing what is placed there will immediately go forward and use it. If the mime has been satisfactory, there should be no moment of hesitation, no need for explanation.

Here are some suggestions which would provide opportunities for group practice in occupational mime. Scenes should not be attempted until there has been some careful practice of individual work.

Suggestions for Group Occupational Practice

INFANTS

It is Christmas morning. The children are divided to represent families in different houses. In one house each child has a stocking to open; in another the postman brings parcels to the door for each one to unpack; in a third the children are giving presents to one another and show what they are. After this they all come to a fourth house to a party, and there is a big Christmas tree; toys of various kinds are taken down by the host and hostess and given to the visiting children; finally Father Christmas himself arrives with a sack of things to add to the others.

*

It is a lovely summer day. The children get up in the morning, wash, dress, and prepare themselves for a day by the sea. They go down to the sands, some dig, some paddle and some try to catch fish in the pools, others sail boats. Presently mothers and fathers bring out picnic lunches, and all sit down to eat. Some men come along, one is selling balloons, another ice-creams and some of the children have one or other. After a little more play they will go home, undress and go to bed.

*

There are Mother pig, Father pig, Auntie pig, Uncle pig and a large family of baby pigs. Father and Uncle decide that they are not very comfortably housed. They call all their friends to help them, and together they build a wonderful house, so strong that no wolf or any other creature could destroy it.

Tired, they all go to sleep contentedly.

*

A naughty little boy is left alone in the house while his mother goes to the shops. He calls in two families of friends who live on either side of his house, and they decide to have some fun; they tie all the furniture together with string, and barricade the dog in the middle of it.

When mother returns she is naturally very much upset.

*

It is winter, the snow is on the ground, the children are allowed to stay out-of-doors instead of going to school. Some make a snowman, others play at snow-balls, others drag one another on sledges, etc. Then it begins to get dark and they are called in to bed.

JUNIORS

The scene is the Doll-Maker's shop. The children are his workmen, and he is in charge of all that happens in the shop. Some are the dolls of various kinds—boy and girl dolls of every nationality, some china, some sawdust, etc. The doll-maker and his helpers finish making the dolls, sewing in the sawdust, painting the faces, putting on their clothes, etc. Others are still busy chopping and carving wood to make wooden dolls, and some are making clothes for these.

When the day's work is done, and the old man and his workers leave the shop, the dolls come to life, but quickly go back to their places when they hear him coming back.

*

The scene is a large kitchen, the cook is busy baking a cake, a woman is washing-up, a boy is scrubbing the floor, a girl is preparing the vegetables, and others are occupied in similar ways. Suddenly there is a disturbance outside and everyone runs out to see what it is. Two children who have been a nuisance to everyone all the morning, stay behind, steal the cake and run away with it. When the cook and the others return there is great trouble.

*

A party of children take a walk in some woods. They come across woodcutters felling trees in a clearing, who let them help with all their jobs. Some make a fire and cook over it, and have a meal with the woodcutters before being taken home by them in the dark.

SENIORS

The scene is a fish quay. Men and women are occupied bringing fish from the boats in boxes, nets, barrels, etc. Some clean fish, others sell them whole. Everyone is busy. Dealers come to buy. Some boats come in laden, others nearly empty. Argument can cause a dramatic incident, or a boat might not return.

Alternatively, the scene could be set on a beach, and the boats would be drawn up by winches.

*

The scene is the fitter's workroom in a big London store. There are a variety of dressmakers at work, pinning, sewing, machining, measuring, etc., according to their particular grade in the workroom. News comes through that no one is to leave the workroom until a search has been made, as everyone is under suspicion for theft.

*

Noah is making his Ark. Various neighbours come and help for a while, but in time each one gives up, and tells Noah he is mad. His three sons, their wives, and Mrs Noah also come and help with finishing touches, though no one works as whole-heartedly as Noah does. He finishes and then the rain comes.

*

A caravan is set by a river. The women of the party are busy with their domestic jobs inside and outside the van. The men are fishing in the river. They have an amazing catch; a fish that needs several of them to help to land it. Some of them fall into the river,—but it was worth it!

ADULTS

The scene is a removal of furniture from a large house into a small one. Four removal men continually bring in furniture; members of the household try to polish the pieces before placing them. Some are washing china, others polishing the floors, others brewing tea. A man is laying carpets and another dealing with electric wiring. Evening comes. Only the darkness causes everyone to stop working.

*

A number of ladies are gathered together at an afternoon bridge party. They play happily; there is an interval when they all have tea. Just as they are resuming their game the party is disturbed by a mouse, which causes such confusion that they give up the game.

*

The scene is a factory. Workers are busily engaged tending the machines. There is a mid-morning break for cups of coffee which they buy from the snack-bar. Work is resumed; there is an accident and the machines have to be stopped.

*

Roman soldiers are throwing dice and gambling round a fire. Some make up the fire, others pour drink, in turn they gamble with cards and dice.

*

The scene is a post office. Behind the counter the officials go through the usual routine with stamps, forms, change, writing, etc.—and on the other side of the counter impatient customers write their telegrams, put their parcels on the scales, go into the call-box and telephone—but nothing hurries the officials.

*

These suggestions are only outlines, anyone of them could eventually be built up into a scene; as they stand they are intended to be for group occupational practice. A scene needs more than this, it must have conflict, and have a climax. It will not be difficult for the group to develop these settings and situations into scenes that have these elements. Let them first work them out clearly as set. They will quickly create characters, and the need to make the drama more powerful will be felt.

VI

ANIMALS AND CHARACTERS

L et us now assume that the pupil has a sure technique, almost second nature. Let the pupil now concentrate on interpretation. This is a more difficult matter than using a set of tricks. It is a focusing of the entire nature to become the thing or person mimed. In this way he will be able to transform and transcend himself and become someone else. Only this is true characterization.

Actors are often tempted to employ 'stagy' tricks: to stoop to represent old age, to hold the lapels of a coat for a Victorian father, to use any superficial act to *represent* a type; but great actors renew their minds continually and use their imagination so fully, that their drama seems to be as true as real life.

In imagining, few exercises help the young and adult pupil more than the pleasing, but not easy, exercise of imagining himself or herself to be an animal. All have observed animals, none can really know them, but pupils who have gone through the preceding exercises will find that they have attained the power of seeming like one when called upon to do so. The body being by now well prepared for this, all we need to do is to concentrate so deeply that the outward showing is like sleep-walking in that the feeling seems to take possession of the movement.

ANIMALS

Let the class sit well-spaced on the floor, no one touching another, and follow these instructions:

Shut your eyes excluding everyone and everything about you; as far as is possible in a sitting position, relax and empty your mind. Now think *cat*. Feel as you sit there that your spine is becoming supple, that from the top of your head all down your spine to the tip of your tail you are sinuous and lithe. Think round your body. Feel as you sit and stare at the world that you are a rather superior being; blink, half-close your eyes, and stare sleepily into the fire. Feel conscious of the top of your head as someone strokes it and you move slightly. Feel the change in your ears when they listen or relax. Your whole face expresses your feelings, even your whiskers, and when you yawn we see your teeth and that tongue that laps milk so easily. Be aware of the soft fur under your chin, and all along your back, your flanks, and underneath you. Again mentally follow your tail to its tip and know its strength. Then think of your legs, back and front, and the soft pads on your paws, and your claws that show themselves when occasion warrants it. Feel the enjoyment of padding round and round on a soft cushion before you sit down in the best chair, or in another mood the pulling at the table cloth, or playing with a ball of wool. Feel pride in yourself as you busily clean yourself with your tongue, and the way at times you arch your back in anger. The stretching movement you do before you prowl away after being relaxed, and the twining of yourself round either human or table leg. Feel sounds growing inside you, maybe a satisfied purr, or an appealing but timid miaow. You may be angry or excited, you may be hungry or happy, we shall know your feeling by the movement and sound you make. Each of you is a particular cat, a particular colour, and temperament. Go on quietly concentrating on *cat*—and when you feel it taking possession of you, begin to move, and make a sound if you feel you must.

Some of the pupils will probably want to move during the description, *this should be avoided*. The result of it can only be that with part of their minds they will be listening and trying to follow the instructions, and with the other part they will be trying to absorb and act.

Class and teacher will gain more if the description is used as a setting of mood and feeling while the class remain seated, possibly moving the body slightly as the feeling grows. Then when the teacher has finished the description, he should encourage some minutes of silent thought, and let each member judge for himself when he is ready to move; some will naturally want to think longer than others. Do not let them open their eyes until they are just beginning to move, thus they will not be made self-conscious by being aware of what others are doing. It is unusual to find a class that does not respond, and often the feeling will be so strong that the impression is truly a room full of cats!

There will probably be among them one who dislikes the cat or any other animal you may choose. Handled gently, this work can help and not frighten such a child. Explain that he *is* the cat, so there is nothing to mind, except the fact that others may fear him, which is a pity since he has no wish to hurt.

This work is suitable for *any age group* provided it is used at the right moment in the training, when there is a readiness to attempt it; it is not a good idea to start on it until the technical work for the whole has been practised. If there is self-consciousness in the class it arises either because this stage has been attempted too soon, or because the presentation has been faulty. Little ones will of course treat it as a game quite readily. Adolescents will find pleasure in it at the right moment. Adults will be shy at first, but will nearly always find great release and help in it when they have grown accustomed to it. An important point for them to realize is that to feel like a cat it is not essential to start on all fours. The sinuous muscular movement can be imagined in the spine while sitting upright in a chair; the face and neck will alter as the mind works, and with older people this feeling through the body is all that should be expected, though almost invariably there will be among them a number of bright spirits who will want to do more.

The action must be governed entirely by *feeling*; directly the intellect begins to work there is a realization that the legs are the wrong shape and that the human body can never appear like an animal body: once these thoughts have arisen it is difficult to revert to feeling only. The thoughts themselves would, of course, be true, but they are not relevant: the facts could not be disputed, but we are concerned not with facts, but with instinctive feeling. A right feeling will always prompt a right movement. This is so true of acting, too: while we admire a good brain behind characterization, too much 'intellectualizing' often makes instinctive feeling impossible.

Now let the class once again sit well-spaced, and prepare mind and body to be relaxed sufficiently to be possessed by any new impression.

Choose another creature—it may be animal, bird, insect or reptile, wild or domestic—and treat similarly to the cat. Take time, and speak to the class in terms of "You are . . ." rather than "It is . . ."; this helps them to become the creature, instead of being, as it were, an objective onlooker. If a wild creature has been selected it often helps to describe the setting—jungle, swamp, river, or whatever it may be; but avoid the temptation to turn the class into a natural history lesson, or you will again impede the flow of feeling. The description is all-important and will make or mar the class.

After the idea has been absorbed and two or three animals have been 'felt' in this way, give the class the opportunity to concentrate in their own time, and without direction from the teacher, on any creature they choose. This gives a sudden feeling of freedom, and nearly always there will be surprisingly interesting results. Do not worry at this stage if you are not exactly clear what they are all representing; it does not necessarily mean they are bad, and if they are bad, no good will come from drawing attention to it. The important factor is that they are now developing their own ideas with intense concentration of the right creative kind, and there is no attempt to copy other people.

Later, when the class is more used to this work, no harm will be done by guessing what each one has become. They in turn can quickly join in and help to speed up the guessing of the last few; do not leave one or two struggling alone at the end.

It should be understood that this development will take place over a series of classes; it would be tiring to work on these themes for too long at a time.

The next development is to ask a member of the class to do the describing. This will refresh everyone, and if you select one with capacity in this direction first, it is sure to succeed; then ask others. Very soon members of the class will themselves suggest that they would like to try. In time let them all have a turn. Individuality will keep the interest of the class alive, and they will become rightly critical of one another's efforts, and will know what constitutes a helpful description and what kind of description presents them with a difficulty. Co-operation and general discussion help a group to work constructively together, and much freedom is gained by them. Even those who have not so much gift in performance may be able to come into their own in discussion or through their descriptive ability. Quite apart from mime itself, this work is of immense value with children, since directly there is desire and competition to be given the chance of describing an animal, the child frequently forgets personal difficulties and inhibitions about speech, and eagerly takes the chance of leadership,—the fact that words are now the medium is forgotten, and a great advance in personal expression is made. This then is of real value in education; helping to make the child expressive and vital.

Thinking again of dramatic expression, it will soon be realized that being a particular animal is not enough. Animals vary even as humans vary, though in a lesser degree. The reasons for their variability are often found in circumstances just as ours are. Another exercise then will be to select a particular animal that the class would like to be. Being this animal let them first try walking slowly, and then move more rapidly, so that they find what difference in feeling there is in the same creature when the rate of movement varies.

Imagine they have selected a Fox:

Let us see the fox lying at rest in his lair, unmolested and content.

Now let us see the difference when he is young and playing, almost like a big dog, happy and free.

Now let us see him running for his life, hunted by the hounds, frightened and alone, looking about for a hole in which he can hide from the huntsmen.

Now again he is close to his home, but he is guarding the vixen and the young cubs, suspicious if anyone comes near; ready to be fierce in being protective.

In another mood, he is alert, ready to attack, scenting danger.

Now it is late evening, he is out hunting, stealing fowls from the farmyard, looking for food everywhere.

Now he is wounded, and struggling because of his wound, trying to get to safety in a miserable plight.

Let us see him now when he is fascinated by something he is watching. Perhaps he is watching a man or, maybe, a snake, and he is afraid. Maybe it is a fire made round a camp to keep wild creatures away. It could be another fox, a stranger to him; or another animal, larger or smaller than he is.

Other moods and reasons for these moods will no doubt be suggested by the classes themselves; the variety in choice of creature will of course affect the chosen mood, but there is plenty of opportunity for development on this theme.

Finally, it is worth trying some scenes introducing animals.

Examples

INFANTS

Mr and Mrs Lion—being King and Queen of the forest decide to have a tea-party. They invite all the birds and beasts to join them. Some are rather timid, others flattered, but they all come. The tea-party starts off well, all are on their best behaviour because they are the guests of Mr and Mrs Lion—but . . .

(Let the children finish it in their own way.)

JUNIORS

It is the middle of the jungle, the antelope have come down to the water to drink; they are startled when they see the

F

vultures flying overhead, and, with a great stampede, they move away back to their mountain ledges. There is a soft padding in the leaves and two tigers meet, under their feet insects scuttle to and fro, and in the distance they hear the movement of a herd of elephants. . . .

(Finish as they like.)

SENIORS

The London Zoo. Cages of animals of every kind. Houses for reptiles and for lions. Water for sea-lions. Elephants and camels meekly carrying children up and down, always covering the same track.

Visitors come and peer and throw buns to them all. . . .

(Finish as they like.)

ADULTS

It is a circus ring. Here is the equestrian with his beautiful prancing ponies who react to his command; then comes the bare-back rider, the performing seals and elephants, the lion tamer with his lions, as well as the clown who will, of course, be there. . . .

(Finish as they like.)

*

There are plays like *The Wind in the Willows*, *The Insect Play*, *Noah*, and *Under the Sycamore Tree*, with ample opportunity for animal characterization, and they are so often played 'straight' with no real attempt at animal quality.

Mime plays could well be adapted from Kipling's *Jungle Books* which give infinite character work in animal life, and provide all the conflict and climax which drama needs.

It will now be found to be quite a good plan to let the

class have the experience of concentrating on nature and inanimate objects, and see if they can feel them so strongly that they convey something of their character. Tell them that it was said of Garrick that "he could act a grid-iron"!

Let the student concentrate and try to feel as if he were being transformed into *a tree*. This does not mean that he raises his arms to look like branches—nothing as external as that—although if he wants to do so ultimately there is no reason why he should not. It does mean that he must think and feel and use his imaginative powers, so that the translation seems to take place, and he is possessed of the feeling without knowing how.

Let him feel in the same way:

> a bush
> a fern
> a blade of grass

feel their vulnerability to the sun and the rain, the wind, the storms, cold and heat, dark and light, as well as to people and animals around them. In the same way he can feel himself being transformed into:

> the sun
> any of the elements

Then inanimate objects like:

> an ancient moss-covered wall
> a rocky cliff

Develop into scenes that introduce all these ideas mixed with human life.

A good setting for infants and Juniors would be

> Under the Sea

Some would choose to be rocks, some sea-weed, others star-fish, crabs, octopus, fish of all kinds, or even mermaids and mermen.

Seniors could set their scene in

An old castle

giving opportunities for ruins, relics, plants, ghosts, knights in armour, mists, etc., as well as the modern tourists.

The average adult will be a little shy of this imaginative work, and should be led to it by gentle degrees, not rushed. Dramatic students will be quite at home in the medium.

A further exercise in the same range of expression is for each member of the class to imagine he is a *sculptor* and to create his work of art. As he does so, the work should become clear. The development is that each one should then

Be the statue he has modelled

He must again feel and concentrate as intensely as possible, and then imagine he is given life. Let the statue grow and be; let it have the soul and life the sculptor had thought of in his imagination.

Here is the feeling first of an inanimate object followed by that of the same object infused with life.

CHARACTERS

When sufficient self-knowledge has been gained through acting the life of the animals, plants, and inanimate objects, then it is time to develop the process further, and use what has been learnt to build up human characterization.

Before doing so, the obvious stepping-stone is to think of two-legged creatures, and, in particular, the monkey—being nearest to man! This is comparatively easy to most people, and a scene in the monkey house is always the greatest fun.

The same way of working can now be applied to human characterization. Instead of descriptions, it may be found to be more valuable to ask a series of questions, allowing time for the pupils to answer themselves mentally, but they must not answer orally. In this way character can grow from individual thought and feeling and will not be dependent on imitation, or on type representation.

Again let the class sit, or be comfortable in any way they like, and prepare themselves to concentrate so that they can become submerged by some character other than their own. The chosen character-type must, of course, suit the age of the class, but I think that this is so obvious that it is unnecessary to give different examples for each age group. Here is an example of the sort of help that the teacher might give. (Dots indicate pauses for the class to think and feel silently.)

You are a *beggar*. You are in a busy city; your age is forty. . . . . . Are you male or female? . . . . . . Are you disabled in any way or are you perfectly well? . . . . . . Or do you act a part, and take on another when you leave your begging behind? . . . . . . How long have you been begging? . . . . . . Do you make much money? . . . . . . Where do you live? . . . . . . What are your likes and dislikes? . . . . . . What do you like to eat? . . . . . . What do you do with the money you have? . . . . . Have you any friends . . . or relations? . . . . . . Think more about yourself and your present life. . . . . . Now cast your mind back to when you were a child, think of your home and family, your school, your young life, your dreams and ambitions. Did you do a job? . . . . . . Think on to the last ten years, of all that has happened until today. . . . . . Now look ahead . . . . . . what lies there? . . . . . . Imagine for a moment that you can see your future lying before you until the end of your life. . . . . . Back to the present again. There you are in your city street. How are you dressed? . . . . . . Where did your clothes come from? . . . . . . What form does your begging take? . . . . . . What is the weather like? . . . . . . What success are you having? . . . . . . What sort of people are passing by and how do they treat you? . . . . . . What do you feel like—is your life a happy one, what is your attitude to all the folks around you and to life in general? . . . . . .

Think quietly for a while; when you feel you are a beggar, begin to move, and make any appropriate sound if it helps you.

*

An exercise such as this helps the class to think constructively, and usually brings good results. Some may object and want to be told more definitely what to think, as they were in the first instance with the cat. By this time, that initial practice should have made the class ready to welcome the opportunity to develop their own ideas, but if some are not yet ready, it is easy to give a fuller description and then to return later to this more advanced method.

Characters such as beggar, a blind man, a typist, a giant, a witch, etc., can be filled out and developed by the individual in this way. Another development can be to describe more specific characters which the class might know, having studied or read the play from which they are taken. Here is an example:

You are a mischievous sprite; your name is Puck. You are the chief attendant spirit on Oberon—the King of Fairyland. You take pleasure in practical jokes, and love to laugh at people's confusion and misfortune, which you yourself have usually caused. You can cover hundreds of miles in a second, passing invisibly through the air faster than any jet. You can disguise yourself as you choose, sometimes as a flower or a leaf, sometimes as an animal,— but at heart you are a mischievous little boy, and often have to be kept in order by your master. No one knows what you eat or how you live; you are of the fairy kingdom and the forest is your hiding-place although the whole earth is yours. You live for ever; you play with the fairies and with other elves when you are not busily employed by Oberon. You are sometimes sorry for your pranks, and you really like the people whom you tease. Oh! the joy of your feelings! The fun of being able to spring into the air and stay there, to settle on a bird's back and whisk over the sea, and then to dive down among the mermaids, until you are caught by Neptune and sent flying back to your own kingdom and your own master! Then perhaps, you trudge the last part of the way pretending to be an old cart-horse until you meet a poor old lady who needs help, and you guide her safely home at night; then off again for some more elfish nonsense. You little green spirit! You are Puck!

*

Again a few moments of silent thought, and then they will start with their own conception of this well-known character. We need not, of course, be limited to Shakespearian characters. Innumerable plays, suitable to every age, lend themselves to this treatment. This way of working will avoid stereotyped imitations, and any danger of the teacher's ideas being implanted, therefore the acting will be sincere. It will also mean that the method can be used by the pupil when he is left to himself. Thus he becomes independent in thought; a very important point. No teaching is good if the pupil in the end relies on the teacher.

The teacher will follow the same process as was used with

the animals. He will describe various characters and then more specific people, from play or book, sometimes giving a detailed description, more often making use of the questioning method. Then still following the same idea, ask members of the class to describe or question, which will again develop thought, interest, and discussion, and benefit everyone.

A further development will be to choose a character and to consider differences of mood related to circumstance, and the effect of other characters on this one—the pupils always trying to translate themselves with truth into the physical and mental feeling of the person.

Finally, scenes which provide opportunity for characterization are a useful practice.

Examples:

INFANTS

The scene is a park; it is a sunny day and many people are passing to and fro. There are seats and chairs, litter-baskets, grass where games are played, and a large pond for those who want to sail boats. All sorts of people congregate there because of the sunshine.

(Give this setting to the children in whatever way they can best follow it—let them decide what kind of person they will be before they begin, so that they can think about it, then let them meet one another and play together, and quite probably some climax will occur. For them it should be just a game, so the performance side doesn't matter at all.)

JUNIORS

You have all gone by coach for the day to Windsor Castle, and you are queueing to see the Queen's Dolls' House which is in one of the rooms. You may be any person in the party; grown-ups and children of all sorts go to see this beautiful dolls' house. When you finally get in, you walk all round four sides of it, and then come out again; then all sit on the seats looking at the view, and have a picnic lunch. Show your reaction to the people around you. Finally board your coach for the return journey.

Take time to think about your characters before you begin the scene.

SENIORS

The characters in this scene are the parents and friends of a young couple at an elaborate cocktail party given in honour of their engagement. At the end of the evening, just as the announcement is to be made, it is discovered that the young man is missing.

ADULTS

The scene is the foyer of a theatre. The play is a modern comedy. This is the moment before it opens, when some are still buying tickets, others hurriedly finding theirs; some wait patiently for late friends; some arrive together—an excited or a bored party; some unexpectedly meet people they know, and so on. Behaviour varies a little according to the clothes being worn, which again depends on where their seats are in the theatre. After a time the bell rings, and there is a general sense of hurry not to miss the opening of the play.

The teacher will find that all sorts of incidents crop up in such a situation. He can encourage them to come about as a result of character and circumstance, without forcing.

Insist that the pupils think about the characters inwardly before starting the scene.

All these scenes could be pure mime if there has been sufficient practice in it. For those who have not done so much mime, it may be easier to improvise words; provided they come readily, there is no harm in using them. The danger is that the speech may become more important than the movement, which, at this stage, would be a pity.

An amusing experiment in this branch of the work is to compare animals and human beings. I would urge, however, that this should only be used sparingly and not be done until after the rest of the work I have suggested here is to some extent mastered. If this other development comes too soon, serious study will be interfered with.

Scenes will grow from this too:

A group of twittering little birds will develop into a gossipy *women's meeting*. Lions and tigers, with an occasional laughing hyena will be perfect in a *gentlemen's political club*!

To some extent all of us behave differently in differing circumstances and with different people: the psychological effect of one person on another must certainly be considered in building a character. This point is fairly obvious. It is perhaps not quite so obvious that people are different at different *hours of the day*. Part of this difference is dependent on their occupations, part on their habits of eating and drinking, part on their leisure-time occupations, and part on innate temper and temperaments.

An exercise then to add to others that have already been used (not to replace them) is to build a character as far as possible, then show the same person at:

7 a.m.   11 a.m.   3 p.m.   6 p.m.   9.30 p.m.   11.30 p.m.
or whatever hours you prefer to select, or possibly also on different days of the week. It will often be quite revealing,

and can be applied to any and every character. Possibly it might even be more real to a group if they first analysed themselves in this way.

There is also usually a difference between people who are doing a job, and the same people off-duty.

Examples:

A waitress	A Member of Parliament
A clerk	An engine driver
A chauffeur	A saleswoman
A queen	A hairdresser

The class will no doubt have other suggestions.

To little ones, character work can only be a game of 'let's pretend', and although they have an infinite capacity for pretending, they do not normally show a great deal of difference in movement; their knowledge is slight, and their imagination is sufficient to satisfy the needs of the game. One will say "I'm a bee", and you will hear him buzzing and there will be some movement. A few minutes later the same child will say "Now, I'm a crab", and the other children will accept him as a crab whether his movement changes recognizably or not. There is no reason to intrude on this natural play, only to add to its pleasure by suggestion; but it is clear that actual 'character' work is not desirable at this level, although animals may prove valuable. Children who are a little older are more aware of people and circumstances, and can work slowly along the lines I have indicated.

It is of even greater importance that seniors and adults should be trained by these slow, simple, honest methods, to ensure that the character shall not be externally put on, like a cloak, but shall be truly created from within.

VII

REACTION

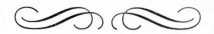

Until now exercises have been chosen in order to give the individual a control of body, mind, and imagination. But no one can live in complete isolation: there is also relationship, which implies action, and what we may call re-action; the clash or agreement that comes from the meeting of wills or minds.

It is a good thing to cultivate natural response through the medium of mime, and for drama it is essential.

Care is needed in dealing with response; to be over-responsive is to over-act. The key-word that all actors and all mimes must remember is *economy*, and if another word should be remembered alongside it, I would say it is *stillness*. As life is movement, and mime is movement, this may seem to be a contradiction, but it is not. Stillness does not mean deadness; there is still breath and life, and in stillness a character may be intensely expressing with every muscle and feature. This is one of the most difficult parts of this art to learn; people are so afraid to take enough time over a movement, and are afraid to conclude one movement and let its effect be 'telling', before passing on to another; then their expressions become blurred instead of having a clear line. They tend to feel that they are not miming if they are not moving, but only that inner urge through the whole body will make the stillness *speak*.

This does not mean that *slowness* must come from stillness. The silence must have the tense purpose of the tiger or snake, not the sleepiness of the sloth or Koala bear.

Breathing has a major part to play in this, as it inevitably follows the emotion and changes with every mood if the feeling is real.

Inexperienced mimes will almost always make the mistake of doing two or three small actions, where one decisive one would have been enough. It takes time to appreciate the need for economy, but it is necessary to realize it, and to feel that every movement, however small, matters. The raising of an eyebrow, the movement of one finger should be telling in themselves. Stillness in the midst of movement has the effect of silence in the midst of noise.

Response can be made to an inward feeling or to an outside stimulus; to something expected or unexpected, to people or to circumstances. The five senses, touch, sight, smell, taste, and hearing will almost always bring a natural response. Many valuable exercises for any age-group can be evolved from this theme.

e.g.   Touch something and respond in feeling or action
      See something and respond in feeling or action
      Smell something and respond in feeling or action
      Taste something and respond in feeling or action
      Hear something and respond in feeling or action

Examples:

TOUCH

Infants	*Juniors*
A teddy bear	A Cat
Prickles	Honey
A worm	Chocolate melting in the sun

Seniors	*Adults*
A sharp knife	A road drill
A canary	A fur coat
Cellotape	A wasp

SIGHT

Infants	*Juniors*
A bunch of balloons	Waves
A car	A monkey
A baby sister	A new dress

Seniors	*Adults*
A ghost	A football match
A whirlpool	A cigar
A head-mistress	A mountain

SMELL

Infants	*Juniors*
A bunch of roses	A field of clover
Soap	The sea
New-mown hay	Newly-baked bread

Seniors	*Adults*
A cow-byre	Burning
Gas	Scent
Fresh paint	A rotten egg

TASTE

Infants	*Juniors*
A banana	Liquorice
Chocolates	Coca-Cola
Milk	Rice pudding

Seniors	*Adults*
Raspberries and cream	A caramel
Medicine	Champagne
Peppermints	A fish bone

HEARING

Infants	*Juniors*
A kitten miaowing	A waterfall
Thunder	A cricket
Someone calling your name	Distant guns

Seniors	*Adults*
A dog barking	Seagulls
A gramophone playing	An aeroplane breaking the sound barrier
An explosion	Schoolchildren in a playground

Quite a number of examples that will evoke response in all parts of the body have already been given in Chapter III. Many other examples could of course be added, as almost everything one does is in some measure a response.

Other Exercises for Response

INFANTS

You are playing in a sand-pit—a strange dog comes and sniffs around, but he goes away and leaves you in peace.

You are watering your garden with a big can, and you soak yourself as well as the garden.

You are enjoying yourself, and you are told to go to bed.

You break one of your favourite toys.

You see a spider on the wall.

JUNIORS

You have built a sand castle with a moat and you are hoping the sea will come into it. You stand on the top and wait,— it comes in more quickly than you thought, and nearly washes it away.

You are looking for fish in a pool, and you find a crab.

You have gone out when you were told not to, and it begins to snow.

You are away from home, and you receive a letter from your mother, or from a member of your family.

You see a caterpillar crawling over your foot.

SENIORS

You have just started in your first job, and you are sent for by your employer.

You are on your way to a garden party in your best clothes, and you are caught in a sudden cloud-burst and thunder-storm.

You are staying with a relation who collects beautiful china. By accident you knock a piece off a shelf and it breaks.

You receive a letter telling you that you have passed an examination.

You see the door open silently, and no one behind it.

ADULTS

You are lying on the beach on a very hot day; you go to sleep and when you are awakened by the waves reaching you, you find you are cut off by the tide.

You are out to dinner with someone of importance, and you burn your mouth badly with your soup.

You are waiting at the station to meet someone whom you dislike; the train is held up by fog, and while you are waiting, a great friend arrives whom you haven't seen for some months.

You receive a telegram,—show whether the news is good or bad.

You hear footsteps and you thought you were alone in the house.

I will now suggest some *phrases* which should come to life through the natural mimed response of the individual. The same phrase will lead to a different reaction with each person who hears it, because each has his own response to give. Let the responses be slow enough to show real thought. A quick facility and forced reaction sometimes occurs in this exercise, which is quite opposed to the intention of this teaching. They should sit quietly and slowly let the thought have its effect—and on no account introduce speech gesture.

The phrases will begin with one of the following:

> "I hear . . . "
> "I think . . . "
> "I know . . . "
> "I am given . . . "

Let the class listen to the phrase, then make their own reactions in movement.

Classes will enjoy thinking of phrases to set their companions for reaction, but here are some examples to set them on the way:

INFANTS

I hear a little mouse talking to its mother.
I hear a cuckoo.
I hear a band.

I think my mother is going out, and I am going too.
I think there is an elf under that tree root.
I think you are a naughty boy.

G

I know you have my doll.
I know there is some jam in that cupboard.
I know what I'm going to do!

I am given a present I don't want.
I am given a rubber ball.
I am given a slap.

JUNIORS

I hear a ship's siren in the distance.
I hear someone talking about my birthday present in the next room.
I hear drums beating in the distance.

I think you are cross with me.
I think I have sprained my ankle.
I think they have seen us.

I know that is an owl hooting.
I know! I am going to draw a picture.
I know you don't like me.

I am given a piece of cake, but it has a dead beetle in it.
I am given a lovely iced drink.
I am given a baby to hold.

SENIORS

I hear wolves, and they are coming closer.
I hear a tap dripping in the bathroom.
I hear someone singing under the window.

I think that is the murmur of a running stream.
I think that you spent a long time doing this.
I think they are coming to take me prisoner.

I know he was innocent.
I know we must go and cut the corn while it's fine.
I know my dog would not bite yours.

I am given a letter from someone I
I am given a hundred lines to write
I am given a horse and harness.

ADULTS

I hear by telephone that my wife has tv
I hear the silence on these hill-tops.
I hear the rats in the wainscot.

I think there is a snake in the grass.
I think this meat is bad.
I think you are guilty.

I know you meant to meet her here.
I know that was an avalanche.
I know it was very cold in the sea.

I am given news of my son's imprisonment.
I am given a letter of apology.
I am given a part in a play.

Another development, which is the absolute opposite of
the inward concentration learned in Chapter VI but none
the less valuable as an *additional* practice, is to react in movement *immediately* without a second's pause, to whatever
enters the mind when a word is spoken.

e.g. *Fire*

Everyone has an immediate reaction; to some the movement
will be an abstract interpretation of flame with rapid
rippling movements; to others it will be the character in
'The Bluebird'; another will move quickly manipulating
imaginary hoses, etc., as if a house were on fire; or again,
someone will visualize sitting by a fire at home, and another
will think of a camp fire, etc. The point of interest is that
with every fresh word, there will be a number of individual
reactions, no two being alike.

...me examples to use:

...ants	*Juniors*	*Seniors*	*Adults*
*...*ormouse	Cosy	Plague	Rumour
Ball	Cook	Lightning	Fever
Slowcoach	Water	Freedom	Misfortune
Bedtime	Adventure	Jester	Courage
Sunday	Gipsy	Fate	Love-lorn

It matters very little what the word is, as almost any word brings a response, but to start with a word having definite and clear possibilities is a good idea.

Then there is the reaction of one person to another to be considered.

Divide the class into pairs

Let each couple start as far from one another as possible, then let them walk until they meet, and react.

Probably the teacher may have to suggest at first whether the meeting is unexpected, pleasant, unpleasant, awkward, opportune, exciting, amusing, nerve-racking, dangerous, etc.—but here is opportunity for spontaneous feeling in a given situation.

It should ultimately be possible to meet without preparing the way, one of the two reacting to the behaviour of the other. This makes for flexibility and alertness in response.

The same exercises can be played as characters; the characters will have to be clear if the partner is going to be able to react suitably. This is quite an advanced exercise, and comes almost out of the realms of mime into acting exercises and spoken drama—and almost certainly a mime scene can develop freely out of the characters evolved by the class.

It will be found that when a reaction is made, of whatever

kind, the whole body momentarily changes. Whether the cause is happy or sad, there is actually a physical reaction which affects breathing, the surface of the skin, and the temperature of the body. The amount of change will depend on the physical state of the person, and the degree of the emotion, but some change is bound to take place.

The understanding and acceptance of relationship give the student greater flexibility, easier readjustment, and quicker response. This is true of all life, and for that very reason is essential in mime, for mime must have basic truth.

In working out reactions and relationships the pupil will discover his own motives, his own thoughts, and this knowledge will help him to liberate himself so that a transformation can occur at will.

VIII

CROWD WORK

We can assume that the classes have now absorbed some basic technique, some ability to concentrate, and have learnt through concentration to feel their way into characters other than their own; then to feel those people's reaction to, and relationship with, other people and things around them.

All this is essential before they can make any contribution in a crowd.

If any imagine that they can hide in a crowd, they are wrong; each individual has to play his part with integrity, and one person not doing so is a drag, and can ruin the whole.

There must be a common purpose and a unified will. This does not smother individuality, but achieves collective relationship.

Technically, it is important for each person to realize that the onlookers will find the picture dull if the same group of players use the same positions on the stage every time they reappear. This sounds very obvious, but it is surprising how often it will happen. People are apt to take the easiest way, and use the space nearest their entrance, and it calls for quite considerable courage to move across a stage to the far side! Each character, therefore, should be given some training in covering as much space on the stage as possible. Then, if a number of people all do the exercises together—covering space, going in several directions, having the courage to leave their entrance and their favourite spot—there will be a natural criss-cross effect which gives an appearance of the natural movement of a mass of people. This sort of exercise must quickly be given some purpose, or none of the players will feel it is sensible.

For this, a scene at Marble Arch on a Sunday evening, with crowds moving from one orator to another, would give a fulfilment to the technical movement. It will be observed that if it is to appear natural and realistic, there will be a varying rate of movement; this is quite an important point.

This mass exercise will probably demonstrate that within every large group there are a number of smaller ones, and that within these smaller groups the relationship between the individuals must be very real, since it is from this nucleus that the whole scene develops.

If it is to develop successfully there will be need for great concentration and understanding, great economy, and real selflessness. It is so easy to steal unintentionally the attention of the audience at a moment when it should be focused on someone else. A sudden swift movement, a big gesture, or a look in the wrong direction, will all serve to do this. The eyes, especially, are so telling in mime and in acting, and the player who knows how to receive an impression, and hold his thought in his eyes, *before* either speech or movement, has great power.

Eye-direction is too important to be misused and must help to focus the attention of an audience wherever it is needed. If a crowd all rivet their eyes on one person or object, or in one direction, the audience looks at that point without knowing why. In the same way if the crowd looks at an entrance before a character arrives on the scene, the audience will look there also, and the character about to enter is greatly helped. The same device is often used to 'build up' an exit. If one member of the crowd isolates himself and does something entirely different, perhaps looking in quite another direction, he will immediately focus attention on himself. A producer of crowd work must be continually on the watch for these points.

A swift movement in a slow-moving group will always attract attention, and so will a slow movement in an excitable and swift-moving scene.

Another way of giving variety of interest and focus to the scene is to arrange steps or rostra in such a way that the characters can make use of the differences of level.

In a set mime play, the producer will probably direct the movement of each player; but much less direction will be required if the players have had some experience in impromptu group work. Then, when it comes to the play, they will be accustomed to free and unconstrained movement, filling the stage well, 'giving' to one another, helping the focus when needed, and making suggestions themselves, (which always helps the life of the production).

When practising impromptu scenes, the classes should still be able to notice whether or not they are part of a good design. Naturally, the character-work and the general impetus and truth of the feeling must not be lost because of this technical point; but as the attention and expectation of the crowd grows, the audience must not be distracted by the awkward appearance of a poor group. The Proscenium Arch (while we still use it) is like a picture-frame, and, as with any picture, the design within it must be satisfying to the spectators. Sometimes, in a crowd, a big sweeping movement may be needed to fill a corner which has become empty because excitement has drawn the group to one side, but no movement should be made without purpose.

It is sometimes useful to stop a scene quite suddenly, asking everyone to hold as a 'still' whatever they were doing or registering at that moment, so that the group realize that no movement can afford to be without intention, and that they may be caught in a 'still' at any time. It is revealing both to the group and to the producer, but this practice should be used sparingly.

Change of mood is difficult to govern in crowd work. It should come from a genuine feeling which runs through the group and is felt and followed. The actors in the crowd are like the members of an orchestra, each of whom must play his part at the right moment, individually vital yet subservient to the whole, not being led away by personal feelings or lack of control to play out of time, out of turn, or out of tune.

Here are some suggestions for practice—starting with reactions between two or three people, following on with small groups, and then larger groups or crowds:

INFANTS

TWO OR THREE TOGETHER

Peter Pan searches everywhere for his shadow. Wendy wakes up and sees him, finds the shadow and sews it on for him. They fly off together.

Cinderella prepares her ugly sisters for the Ball.

SMALL GROUPS

Cinderella tries on the glass slipper; there is great rejoicing from the Prince and annoyance from the ugly sisters.

Buying a pair of shoes at a shop.

LARGE GROUPS OR CROWDS

A childrens' party—refreshments—games, entertainment, etc.

A school picnic—setting out—arriving—eating—playing —returning.

Snow White eats the apple given her by the witch—the Dwarfs arrive and find her, and all their forest friends come too.

JUNIORS

TWO OR THREE TOGETHER

The little mermaid longs for legs. The witch gives them to her, but every step she takes is like walking on knives.

King Midas is given by the gods the gift of the golden touch. He is delighted that all he touches turns to gold. By chance he turns his daughter to gold, and he is grief-stricken. The gods give him the power to undo the spell.

SMALL GROUPS

Sleeping Beauty, surrounded by some members of her Court, wakes up after a hundred years.

Rumpelstiltskin asks the people round him to guess his name and is angry when he finds someone knows it.

Little boys play at hopscotch, also at marbles, in the street. They are given some ice-cream and eat it·

LARGE GROUPS OR CROWDS

Waiting in a queue outside a cinema or children's theatre on a Saturday morning.

A child has run away from school, and suddenly comes in among his friends, having been found in a wood.

A Scene 'At the Fair'.

SENIORS

TWO OR THREE TOGETHER

A mother and father are at breakfast. Their daughter arrives very late, and is reprimanded by father from behind his paper. The daughter opens a parcel and finds it is a banned book sent her by a friend. Mother disapproves and confiscates it; the daughter is angry, smashes a piece of crockery and leaves the room.

A peasant girl is gathering sticks with an old woman. The girl's arm is paralysed, and she cannot work fast enough to satisfy the old woman, who leaves her. While alone, the girl sees a vision, her arm is restored and the old woman on her return is converted to kindness.

SMALL GROUPS

A lady insists on completing her purchase and buying a hat just after closing-time; the assistants are trying to clear up, but the customer keeps them busy.

In a railway carriage. On one side of the window is a fresh-air fiend. Opposite is a very smart well-dressed lady; there are other characters in the compartment who take sides in the battle between these two.

It is rehearsal night for the village orchestra. There are only a few instruments; they are enthusiastically practising for their concert.

LARGE GROUPS OR CROWDS

Waiting to see the Queen in a large crowd outside Buckingham Palace. There are police, of course, and a mixture of people from far countries in the crowd.

It is the 'rush-hour' in a little café close to a station and people are anxious to catch trains. The waitresses are very overworked and their tempers are frayed.

A suburban 'bus-stop. Several full 'buses have passed, and a woman in the queue decides to hail a taxi. While she is doing this, another 'bus appears, the rest of the crowd board the 'bus, and she is left behind, for the taxi was occupied.

ADULTS

TWO OR THREE TOGETHER

A scene at the hairdressers, or the barbers.

A newly-wed couple go to have their photograph taken. The photographer takes great pains setting them in position, etc. Just as he is about to take the picture, one of them sneezes and upsets the pose. He starts again. When all is again set, a wasp buzzes round and disturbs them. They are so upset that they rush away without having the photograph taken.

SMALL GROUPS

A prisoner is in his cell. Gaolers outside his door drink and gamble. He is called to his trial.

Hollywood managers are auditioning chorus girls and variety artists. Some are chosen. The former leading lady is jealous of the new one, slaps her face and walks out. The new one makes herself popular with the leading manager.

Two nannies are in a park, each with two children, one of which is a baby in a pram. One of the children teases the baby, dangling a worm in front of it. The nursemaids quarrel.

LARGE GROUPS OR CROWDS

In a fashionable shop there is a fashion parade. Men and women are having tea and discussing the dresses, and the models.

A big liner is reaching its destination. Most of the passengers are on deck. It is apparent that they have mixed feelings, according to whether they are reaching home, or arriving in a foreign land.

In a Bar Parlour, a barmaid is serving drinks—and flirting. Following a commotion outside, an injured man is carried in. She makes her way through the crowd to give him brandy, and recognizes the husband she had deserted years before.

A crowd of students in a street are demonstrating for a topical cause.

*

So far attention has been given to group feeling concerning normal people in a crowd. Now it will help the mass feeling to practise abstract mime in group form.

Quite a good way to begin this, is to ask the class to react spontaneously to sounds and rhythms, either human or instrumental. They become accustomed to their bodies following an impulse of feeling, and with the mind controlling what they are doing, they allow that feeling to direct the movement of the body.

For this exercise all the percussion instruments will be valuable, but perhaps the simplest is to beat a large tambour and occasionally to use cymbals to heighten the effect. The rhythm should be varied. Probably at first the effect will be primitive, but by degrees other feelings will emerge, and quite frequently each individual will develop his own little scene. Often there will be something grand and elemental in conception, which can readily be developed into a subject for mass movement.

When there is a feeling of freedom, direct it by asking them to be conscious once again of the pattern of the whole group and the pictorial effect. When this has grown to be a habit, select some elemental themes, and see if the whole group can react individually in their own way, while yet giving a collective whole:

Examples

> The Planets
> Storm
> Clouds
> Earthquake

It may be that good musical accompaniment will be available, which is naturally a great help, but rather than use poor and inadequate music, let the players make their own noises. If there is any feeling against this, do not force it upon them; if you do, they will not then be free. But some classes will be grateful to be allowed to express themselves in sound without restraint.

Another example that will be suitable at this stage is an abstract expression in group form called:

The Evolution of Man

The group huddle together in a heap on the floor, trying to forget they exist, trying to be nothing. Then by degrees they become something else: a moving mass, from which some will become rock, others primitive animals, birds or insects, others plants, until man himself emerges. Good grouping and good feeling will nearly always grow from this exercise, which seems to have a general appeal to all humanity.

Very often classes will themselves suggest starting at an earlier stage and ending later—e.g. by being Ether, and then after having reached man, becoming spirit only. This produces a sense of lightness that is gained in no other way.

Now divide the class into half, and ask one half of the group to express *war*; ask them to move freely and become a still tableau. Then ask the other half to move and mingle among them expressing *peace*, these also becoming eventually a still tableau. Finally, ask them all to move again— preferably without touching one another—and let the conflict arrive at its own conclusion; it may go either way. Having grasped the idea through this rather obvious choice of *war* and *peace* experiment with other abstract conflicts:

> Interest and Boredom
> Order and Confusion
> Stillness and Movement
> Serenity and Worry

Next divide the class into three groups. This time the idea is not one of conflicting emotions, but of progressing from one emotion to another. One group begins by expressing a feeling; a second group enters expressing a second feeling which influences the first group. A third group enters with a third feeling, and the whole class follows this third feeling.

Similarly, divide the class into four groups, and choosing four emotions, follow the same process of progression of feeling. At this point the feelings should be entirely abstract expressions. For example, the individual may represent 'sorrow' *itself* not someone who *is* sorrowful.

Examples

Sorrow changes to *hope* then to *joy*.
Uncertainty changes to *fear* then to *anger* then to *lethargy*.

Now, allow the class to work together again as *one large group*. This time suggest a succession of five or six emotions or states of mind which follow one another, for the whole class to interpret. They will know the order, but will not plan the movement from one emotion to the next. This should happen naturally if their feelings are genuine.

Examples

Freedom, anxiety, bewilderment, captivity, despair.
Tranquillity, rumour, anxiety, terror, grief, resignation.

Music again will help very much, but it is more than likely that by this time the students will be wanting to express themselves vocally and it may help their feeling to do so. Do not mix the two kinds of accompaniment. It would be futile to suggest sounds to the class, but here is an indication of the kind of sound that might be expected from:

Tranquillity—a vague serene humming
Rumour—a hissing or buzzing of voices
Anxiety—questioning or doubtful inflection of sounds without words
Terror—screams
Grief—sobs
Resignation—a slight sighing

Now is probably the right moment to allow these abstract emotions to become personal, and be given reasons.

Ask the class to suggest a theme and a possible development for some of these emotions. There will be many and varied ideas.

Here is a possible suggestion:

Tranquillity—A small village in Central Europe is happy, and the people go about their daily work without fear or trouble.

Rumour—News comes that troops have been seen gathering on the borders.

Anxiety—If it is true, what are they to do?

Terror—Without further warning, armies arrive and invade the village, burning and pillaging as they go, leaving destruction behind them.

Grief—Homes and loved ones have been lost in the invasion.
Resignation—Time passes, life must go on for those who are
left, and the village be re-built for the next generation.

Now here are some suggestions of abstract scenes for
practice.

INFANTS

A group of trees. When night comes and the moon is high,
they come to life and dance together; but no human ever
sees them or discovers their secrets.

One evening a little girl is playing on the sands when
everyone else has gone. She is delighted to find that the
waves each have a spirit, and that they rush out of the sea
and play with her. Some are rollicking and boisterous,
others are more timid and slow. They run back to the
sea when she goes, promising to meet her again another
day.

(A similar idea could be applied to other aspects of nature,
provided it is not over-used.)

You are what is called 'still life'. A potato, an orange, a
silver tray, a Dresden statue, a jug, and a dead fish. Someone
is painting you in a picture; when the artist goes, you all
come to life.

Half of you are a smouldering fire which is gradually
spreading from bush to bush. The other half are a waterfall
which is running swiftly into a river. The fire and the water
meet and clash, and the fire is vanquished.

JUNIORS

One of you is a witch. She is brewing a spell in her cauldron.
The rest are the spell, which gradually grows and shows
itself.

H

Clytie, the nymph, is in love with Apollo, the Sun-God. Daily she watches his journey across the sky and hopes he will notice her. He does not. The spirits of nature are kind to her, and she becomes a sun-flower.

Express what you feel in movement when a sound is suggested to you and create a scene round it. E.g. drums, a bell, breaking glass, a bleat, guns.

The God Mercury brings Pandora a box and instructs her not to look inside it. When he has gone, the temptation is too strong for her, and she peeps in. At once all the Evils spring out of it and flood the world. She struggles to shut it, and just before she manages to do so, Hope has escaped also.

SENIORS

Spirits are in torment of every kind. They work together and manage to triumph over the Devil.

Base a scene on any of the following words:
Conscience. Achievement. Sleep. Hostility. Self-aggrandizement.

One of you represents your brain. The others are evil thoughts that come from various places and enter your mind. The brain quells these thoughts.

The spirits of the dead are in Hades. Death enters, then Pluto and Persephone. Orpheus comes to find Eurydice, and she is given to him on condition that he does not look at her. As she follows him she entreats him not to look, but he cannot resist the temptation, turns and sees her. She fades, and he is banished from Hades.

Express what you feel in movement when colours are suggested to you: red, black, blue, purple, green, yellow.

ADULTS

Life and Death struggle for the possession of a beautiful girl. Death triumphs over her body, but Life possesses her soul.

A woman is in misery. Temptation comes to her and tries to persuade her to commit suicide. She struggles and nearly yields, but finally overcomes Temptation.

The scene is a churchyard. It is a moonlight night; bats and owls and the church clock are the only inhabitants. Men gather for a clandestine meeting, and as they are leaving to fulfil their purpose, they are haunted by their guilty consciences.

An artist is starving; he works, but no one wants his pictures. He is visited by Material Necessity, and later by Inspiration. He struggles between the two.

Immanent Will creates the Iceberg. It also creates the *Titanic*. At a given moment in time they come together. The ship sinks, the Iceberg moves on.
(Suggested by Hardy's poem—'The Loss of the *Titanic*'.)

*

In any of these suggestions the abstract concepts may be suggested by one person, or a group of people.

By this time classes will have appreciated that to be part of a crowd is as exciting as any solo performance, that the work is just as arduous but equally rewarding. Each individual contributes to the mass feeling.

IX

IMPROVISATION WITH UTTERANCE

Teachers will find that improvisation with utterance or speech can give their pupils both confidence and control. The actor must be ready to make use of it on occasion when he is faced with an emergency; practice in it will be an addition to all previous mime training, but will never take the place of it.

In improvisation, mime and sound should spring spontaneously as from one source. There can be no success in miming, and then in adding words to fit the mime, nor yet in speaking, and then adding mime to fit the speech. There can be satisfaction only if both happen together, or if one is the inevitable outcome of the other.

This does not mean that all movement must be accompanied by utterance or speech. The situation must be natural and therefore sometimes silent. Most people, when alone, refrain from talking to themselves, though they may occasionally let forth a sigh, a grunt, or an ejaculation.

It is necessary to remember this when improvising solo scenes. I have seen people try to improvise, who—feeling that they ought to be talking—have either uttered all their thoughts aloud—in the form of a soliloquy—or talked to imaginary characters around them. Certainly some have the gift of 'peopling' an empty stage, but these are rare artists, and in scenes where this technique is required, the words are usually of primary importance and the mime becomes secondary. The result will then be a prepared monologue or sketch; this is no longer improvisation.

Improvisation does not need to be taught in the same way to infants and juniors. They talk freely in their natural play, and will be quite ready to express themselves in sounds or in words without feeling awkward or self-conscious.

With these younger children it is important that the mime already learnt should bear fruit and be developed into play-making.

Generally speaking, small children are much more success-ful in their plays when they have been allowed to improvise their own words. A useful beginning is to suggest to a few children who are quite good at mime that they act particular characters, and let them begin a scene, using sounds or words if appropriate; the rest of the class will listen, and directly they see an opportunity for the entrance of another character others will in turn join in and add to the scene.

Examples:

> One child will be a witch
> One child will be a princess
> One child will be an owl

Here are our first three characters. They will probably know how they want to start the scene;—if not, suggest that it is set in a forest; the owl is perched on a branch hooting occasionally and the witch is stooping over her cauldron, muttering to herself as she brews her frightening spells (for she is a wicked old woman). After a few minutes the princess comes along, speaks to the witch and tells her how she climbed over the palace wall to find the golden ball which she had thrown too far, that it was so fascinating outside that she has lost herself and is tired.

Childen will soon develop the theme, and all sorts of characters will join in—fantastic, animal, and human.

The improvising must be very free, but if it is to become their own play the teacher will no doubt need to help by pruning here and developing there, and finally deciding the exact order of entrance, the timing, climax, and conclusion. Having thus reached the form of a play, improvisation must be put aside, and, however young the children, the discipline of the theatre must begin. They have selected their own words, the words must now be accurate; the movement becomes planned to their own design, and must not change, —unless to make an agreed improvement.

Acting now becomes quite a serious business, and they will enjoy it all the more because of this. Teachers are some-times apt to be carried away by free work, improvisation, and what is called 'the play way', so that nothing ever reaches a satisfactory conclusion or makes an artistic whole, and no one learns the meaning of control. In all good dramatic work freedom and control must go hand in hand, and while improvisation is the perfect way for infants and juniors to learn, we must not be content for it to end in a rather poor charade. If we are, then we might as well leave the children to play happily in their own way and without guidance.

The main difficulty in this work however is experienced by seniors and adults, and therefore much of this chapter is written with them in mind. The difficulty seems to be in the transition from mime to words. Explaining to them that there really is no transition does not always help.

I have found that the easiest method is to ask them to think about their own natural behaviour when alone, and after that to suggest the right kind of examples for practice, asking them to do them perfectly naturally, making a sound or saying a word if it would be normal to do so, and not otherwise.

The examples selected should be of such a nature that they will call forth a natural response in sound, probably demanding at first only an ejaculation; then developing others, which bring the natural response of a word, or words. In this way, the class will realize that quite a considerable amount of time may be spent in silent acting, that nothing should be forced or unnatural, and that utterance of some sort, whether in sound or speech, will happen in its proper place.

The teacher will soon find that the examples develop into little scenes. He must realize, that more particularly in teaching this branch of the subject, the selection of example matters. It must be suitable for the class, and must be graded so that the development is sufficiently gradual, and so that they are never made to feel silly, awkward, or self-conscious. Once this happens the work is valueless.

I would, therefore, advocate very strongly indeed that in the early stages (even though we must call them 'solo examples'), the whole class should work together without onlookers. This applies to all mime classes; only gradually, as confidence grows, should any solo work be asked for.

In improvisation there will naturally be exclamations and sounds of all kinds springing from all quarters of the class at different moments; this does not matter, let them go ahead in their own time regardless of one another, thus any foolishness they might have felt if left alone is lost, because the individual movements and sounds appear to merge into one. The experienced teacher grows accustomed to looking at and seeing the individual within the group.

Presently the moment will come for two to improvise together, and then for small groups. It will still be well, to begin with, to allow all the groups to act at the same time. Gradually they will suggest watching each other's scenes, and interest will take the place of awkwardness.

Eventually the whole class can join in a concerted group scene, and having worked from solo scenes, through the small group to this point, they will all be ready and able to contribute to such a scene. Some of the crowd scenes suggested for mime in Chapter VIII could equally well be used for improvisation.

When the class is quite at home in this work, refer back to some of the solo improvisations and ask some members to repeat them alone. If this seems too great an ordeal, do not force it, but let half a dozen do the same scene at one time, then gradually reduce the number until all grow accustomed to the idea. Then allow those who have gifts in this medium to use them for the enjoyment of others, but quick thinking is needed, so some will excel in this, and others will succeed more easily in prepared work. Rightly handled by the teacher, as with all mime, confidence and ease will develop, but wrongly handled, no good will come of any of it, only acute discomfort.

Here are some suggestions of examples that are likely to bring response in sound or word as well as in movement:

Ejaculations

You are: sewing, and prick yourself.

trying to read, but are constantly disturbed by a fly.

putting the finishing touches to your toilet, and just as you are ready, you ladder your stocking.

asleep, and are wakened by an alarm clock.

opening a tin and you cut yourself.

doing up a shoe-lace, and it breaks.

listening to a play, and someone in the ı behind rustles sweet papers.

cooking, and you burn yourself on a hot pan.

walking, and you trip unexpectedly.

taking a cold shower, against your will.

watching a clown at a circus.

seeing the top of a snow-mountain for the first time.

watching a village cinema show, and the projector fails.

out to tea, and you upset your cup in your lap.

dozing in a train, and wake up to find you are moving out of the station where you wanted to get out.

preparing a meal, and the milk boils over.

watching a trapeze artist, and he falls but is caught by the safety net.

watching motor-racing.

sitting quietly, and a mouse runs across the room.

standing on a pavement, and a car nearly runs you down.

walking into the sea on a lovely hot day.

carrying a suit-case, and it opens in a crowded street.

waiting for the curtain to go up on the opening night of a show, and a 'prop' is missing.

Let the class take plenty of time to get into the scene, and build up to the moment of ejaculation. Some examples may not bring an audible response, but the class will be quick to suggest others they like better. Sometimes it works well for them to set exercises of this kind for one another to do.

If some pupils suggest that they never make audible response under any circumstances, let them act the sort of person who might do so; very often the people who make this sort of objection are those who need the freedom that this work gives, more than the rest.

IN TWOS

Two people are:

sitting reading quietly, and there is a sudden clap of thunder.

walking arm-in-arm and one trips.

going into the sea on a cold day; one who is already wet splashes the other, who is not.

pulling a cracker together.

listening to the radio; one smells burning, the other remembers the cake in the oven.

in a street, one is on a ladder cleaning windows, the other walking underneath; the wet cloth drops on his head.

trying the bumper cars at a fair.

standing on the edge of a swimming bath, one pushes the other in.

in a restaurant; one is a waitress who spills the soup down the customer's neck.

SMALL GROUPS

You are watching television—Decide before beginning what the programme is, and remember it is not likely that there would be much talk from you, but sometimes an ordinary reaction that might be audible as sound or words.

You are a family:

at home	at the races
in a tube train	or in any other circum-
at a party	stances you prefer

BIGGER GROUP SCENES

You are waiting in a queue. Let us see and hear the difference in the following circumstances:

> a 'bus queue
> a shop queue
> a theatre queue
> outside a zoo
> a cinema queue

In each case end the scene by passing through a turnstile or door or going inside. It could, however, be equally effective without the entrance, if the characterization is strong enough.

Now other group scenes with utterance should happen quite naturally, following on the suggestion of a title.

Examples:

Before the wedding	Budget day
Bank holiday	On the brink of disaster
Departure	Planets
Nonsense	

Whatever the title, no two groups of people will ever react in the same way, so there will always be variety.

Another idea is to divide a large class into a number of small groups, making each group responsible for part of a continuous scene. Those not taking part can be watching but ready to take their part at the right moment, without any pause.

Examples:
The scene is:

A Snack Bar

Two or three waitresses will remain in the scene throughout—the other groups of different people will arrive at different hours of the day, and with no lull between each. The scenes will be at:

> 8 a.m.—on the way to work
> 11 a.m.—people of leisure
> 1 p.m.—lunch break
> 4 p.m.—tea time
> 7 p.m.—supper
> 11 p.m.—after the theatre

Several different groups can of course enter at one period; this just depends on the numbers in the class.

Similarly, the exercise could be played

a) In an ice cream kiosk
> or
b) On the first day of the sales (the same department throughout)
> or
c) In a hotel kitchen (various shifts of workers)

Now, thinking back to the original ejaculations, some of the class will perhaps be inclined to develop them into little personal scenes. Others may like ideas which are more formed, but which still lend themselves to improvising with utterance.

Here are some suggestions:

1. You are trying to put up a camp bed; it is awkward and stiff and you find yourself doing ridiculous contortions before your efforts have any success.

2. You are sitting in a haunted room just before midnight. You have been told that terrible happenings take place as the clock strikes twelve. Midnight strikes, and you show what happens.

3. You take your little pug dog on a 'bus. You hoped to travel inside but are forced to take him on top, much to your disgust.

4. It is Hallowe'en. You are sitting looking in the mirror imagining you will see your future husband. You see something you didn't expect in the mirror. You show what it is.

5. You decide to lay some linoleum in a small old-fashioned bathroom. While you are struggling to fix it, someone opens the door, and you find yourself entangled in linoleum, half under the bath.

6. You are a maid taking early morning tea to a guest in a hotel. You are surprised that she does not wake when you draw the curtains and light the fire. When you go to the bed you find she has been murdered.

7. You are very poor, and are tempted by something you see in a shop, which you know your mother badly needs. Finding you haven't the money, you slip it into your bag. You leave the shop and you are stopped by a detective.

8. You are listening to a gramophone on a verandah in a hot country. Suddenly you see a snake close by and reailze it is a cobra rearing its head to attack you.

9. You take a turkish bath for the first time—starting off very gaily. Deciding it's not worth it when you arrive at the hottest room, you return rather crestfallen.

Once again after these solo scenes I would end by bringing a whole class together. The practice should have strengthened their feeling of freedom, and they should be able immediately to make an amusing improvisation with words on a subject like:

Camp

starting with the arrival—erecting tents—cooking—fetching water, etc.,—introducing every aspect of mime and coming to the beginnings of play-making. Directly groups begin to invent scenes or plays it will be necessary to add the other ingredients of drama; i.e. not only character, which will be there, but circumstance, conflict, and climax.

X

OTHER COUNTRIES AND OTHER TIMES

Mime can be of benefit to most subjects in the school curriculum, and the mime teacher should help by trying to correlate his illustrations with the year's work. He will be unlikely to set out to teach a scientific subject like geography which requires vast specialized knowledge, but he may help to interest the children by asking them to imagine and mime some of the conditions of life in other parts of the world.

Correlation with the Geography Lesson

Climate will usually be of immediate interest, and the class could well begin with some discussion of heat and cold and their effect on body and movement. They will generally conclude that cold creates contraction and tension, while heat induces expansion and relaxation. Also that cold often brings about brisk movement in order to keep warm, while heat tends to make gentler movement and leisurely action more comfortable; but that the extreme of either might bring life to a standstill.

Here are some exercises developing this theme. They

could be used with any age provided they were appropriately introduced:

Move about imagining that it is:

> a pleasantly warm English summer day
> an unusually scorching English day
> a hot dry day somewhere near the equator
> a day of humid moist heat

Take time feeling the difference between these varying kinds of heat and the way you would react. Then repeat the last two as someone who is accustomed to live in those conditions, and notice if the reaction is different. It almost certainly will be.

Now move about imagining that it is:

> a damp English November day with drizzling rain
> a thick English fog in a city
> a sunny day with snow on the ground and crispness in the air
> further north, colder, greyer, with snow, but no sun.
> nearer the North Pole where nothing lives

Repeat the last two as if you were fully prepared and equipped for such cold, as the members of a polar expedition might be.

Now imagine the effect of other kinds of weather or climatic conditions.

Move as if you were in:

> a very strong wind
> a hail storm
> a snowstorm
> a thunderstorm
> rain
>
> a sandstorm
> a gale
> the terrifying wind at the top of Mount Everest

Let the class now divide into small groups. Each group will now be responsible for making a mime scene which will show a climatic condition or temperature. The scenes should cover as many different parts of the world as possible.

Watching each other's scenes, the class will soon begin to observe how temperature and climate affect behaviour, and as the characters in the scenes begin to emerge an understanding of national characteristics will grow too.

If the children begin to think of too many ideas at once, the mime will become untidy and the results will not satisfy them; that is why this sequence should develop slowly, and concentration on climate and character will be as much as can be carried out satisfactorily at first.

They might then learn something more by considering the countryside in this way:

Show the difference in your feeling as you walk:

on a mountain track	on downs
on a tarred road	on rock
on quicksand	through jungle
on desert sand	

It may be a good plan to repeat some of the scenes which illustrated climates and see if enough consideration had been given to the surface of the earth.

This brings them immediately to modes of transport, always an exciting topic for children:

Imagine you are travelling:

on a horse	in a boat
in a rickshaw	on skis
in a car	on a bicycle
on a mule	in a lorry
on a camel	on a sledge
in a jet airplane	in a train

I

These need considerable skill in mime, but the feeling can be conveyed quite well while remaining on one spot. Consider again if any of these would have helped the scenes, and try to see the sort of countryside in which they might be.

What kind of shelter will these people have? Where do they live?

Show that you are in:

a tent	an igloo
a house	a caravan
a mud hut	a castle

Immediately, in order to show this, the children will want to begin 'doing', so the sort of occupation will become an interest.

Show that you are:

fishing	cotton growing
wine-making	doing factory work
fruit-farming	tea planting
doing basket work	rice picking
sheep shearing	

They will also want to think about the food and drink of other peoples. So they can try examples to show this:

Show that you are eating:

figs	pumpkin pie
macaroni	rice
avocada pears	pickled herring
bamboo shoots	

Show that you are drinking:

vodka	tea
Coca-Cola	sherbert
goats' milk	

What will they wear in other countries and climates while doing various occupations?

Show that you are wearing:

a sari	a mackintosh
Hawaiian straw skirts	a kimono
an Arab's head-dress and robes	a yashmak
an Eskimo's skins	a coat and skirt

I only give examples of variety; naturally the lessons could be directed along particular channels, depending on whether the ways of a special country will be more useful, or a wide variety to set the classes thinking for themselves. They can be encouraged to bring fresh scenes to illustrate various points, and in doing so they will often have to look up and find out information for the scene, which is valuable. They will also become more aware of the different ways of thinking and acting in different parts of the world.

Correlation with the Scripture Lesson

Many of these suggestions can be used as a contribution to the scripture lesson.

Climate, countryside, transport, shelter, occupation, food, and clothes are all applicable. The method of working can be much the same, only in this case the bias will be in a different direction. Characters will now have to stand out strongly against the appropriate background; the people in the stories matter more than their surroundings. The exercise of acting scenes will now be less of a study, the purpose being rather to make the stories more memorable. Perhaps this may not seem to be necessary, but I think it is comparable with little children drawing pictures of stories in Sunday School; only in this way the pictures come to life. Most teachers will have their own ideas about which stories to mime, so a lead is probably unnecessary, but here are a few suggestions:

INFANTS

Noah building the Ark with his family. The animals are collected. The rain comes.

The Nativity. Shepherds and kings visit Mary and Joseph and the Baby in the stable.

JUNIORS

On the Ark. The sending out of the dove, and the return with the olive branch.

Pharoah's daughter, Princess of Egypt, goes down to the Nile with her ladies, to bathe. She finds Moses hidden in the bulrushes, keeps him as her son, calls an Israelite to be his nurse; the child's mother offers herself and is accepted as his nurse.

SENIORS

The return of the Prodigal Son. There is great feasting and great rejoicing.

The parable of the Good Samaritan.

The feast of the Passover, and the Israelites journeying across the Red Sea.

David slays Goliath. Saul is jealous. David plays to Saul. Saul throws a javelin at David, but he avoids it.

ADULTS

The healing of the blind beggar by St Paul.

Adam and Eve eating the apple and being banished from the Garden of Eden.

Two mothers make claim to one baby before King Solomon. He offers to cut it in two. The true parent is recognized because she would rather give up the baby than have it destroyed.

Salome dancing for Herod and demanding the head of John the Baptist.

Correlation with the English Lesson

The English lesson offers such obvious opportunities for mime that there is little need to give space to it.

Most teachers will, I think, agree, that episodes from 'set books' are likely to live more fully in the mind of the young person after being acted. For this purpose it will be wise to concentrate largely on characterization; then revert to the book and re-read the description given by the author, so that there is an incentive to read and an enjoyment in doing so. To the scholar or the more literary child reading will be a habit, but not to all. Here again are some suggestions for scenes:

INFANTS

The story of 'The Tailor of Gloucester' by Beatrix Potter (or others in this series.)

The story of 'The Three Bears' or other fairy stories.

Some of the adventures of 'Tom and the Water Babies'.

JUNIORS

The story of the poem 'Goblin Market' (Christina Rossetti).

Some of the adventures of 'Alice in Wonderland'.

Ulysses and his men land and find the lotus-eaters—some eat the lotus and fall under its spell—Ulysses drags the others back to the boats.

Perseus is sent by the King to slay the Gorgon and bring him its head. He meets Athene who gives him a sword and shield and warns him not to look at the Gorgon. Perseus slays the Gorgon and brings the head to the King, who looks at it and is turned to stone.

SENIORS

The Lady of Shallott sees 'the mirror crack from side to side'.

From *The Pickwick Papers*—Mr Winkle and Sam Weller with their companions on the ice.

'Vanity Fair' and other episodes from *The Pilgrim's Progress*.

An Elizabethan tavern—the death of Christopher Marlowe.

ADULTS

Episodes from the life of Samuel Pepys.

The death of Cleopatra—from *Antony and Cleopatra*.

Mephistopheles shows Dr Faustus the wonders of the world and the beautiful Marguerite—tempting him to sell his soul. He agrees, but when he would keep Marguerite for ever she has to return to Mephistopheles, and Faustus becomes an old man.

Comus brings the lady to his palace and introduces her to Greed, Avarice, Pride, and his other followers. She is made to drink and turns to stone, but is rescued by Sabrina and her brothers.

Correlation with the History Lesson

The history lesson naturally takes us away into other times, and here mime can offer an important contribution.

Infants and Juniors will be interested and excited in the subject because they love stories, and love acting stories; these they should be allowed to mime freely, or develop into their own plays. If some are good story-tellers, a narrative could string together a series of episodes, some of which could be told, some mimed, some acted, or told in verse.

Seniors and adults will need to do (and will enjoy doing) some detailed study of the modes and manners of the times, so that the movement in the scenes is appropriate. In doing the necessary careful study or research, their own knowledge of social history must increase. There are interesting reasons to be found for changes of costume and these are linked with changes of movement. Without at least some knowledge of the social background of the times, 'period' or historic movement is bound to look mechanical and unreal.

Look at the pictures and you will realize that although the human shape always remains the same, it is astonishing how humanity has contrived to alter it by variety of costume. Compare the outline in pictures of:

Julius Caesar, Dante, Richard of Bordeaux, Henry VIII, Charles II, Napoleon *or*

Helen of Troy, Cleopatra, Joan of Arc, Queen Elizabeth I, Nell Gwyn, The Empress Josephine, Queen Victoria.

Studied chronologically, the infinite variety of costume and shape explains itself; one thing evolves from another. Generally speaking, a period of war brings little change except that the clothing becomes more practical or more military; while a period of peace usually brings an interest in dress and more elaboration. Very often the personal foible of a reigning monarch or someone of importance sets a fashion. For example, in James I's reign fashions changed little, because he and his wife were thrifty. The men wore padded clothes, largely because the Scots king (feeling he was in a foreign land, and having the fate of his Mother, Mary, Queen of Scots, well in mind), adopted padded clothes—his courtiers following suit, and so the fashion was set. The weight of the costume obviously affects the movement, so a detailed study of costume is bound to be a help.

Books on historical costume are legion, so I shall not enlarge by giving full costume notes here; but naturally it would be advisable to show pictures of the period to a class, and consider in which way the clothes would affect movement, before starting to build up the atmosphere.

The notes that here follow are no more than a skeleton for further study, but include some points of interest about each period that might be helpful, because of their dramatic significance, in building a historic scene in mime. It will be found, too, that these beginnings will tempt the children to continue research for themselves.

MEDIAEVAL PERIOD
A.D. 1000 *to roughly* 1450

There are few contemporary accounts of the early part of this period, but much information can be gained from the study of carvings, effigies, tapestries, and illuminated manuscripts, and later from stained glass, brasses, and pictures.

By the twelfth century there were books called 'Herbals' which were about plants, also 'Bestiaries' about animals and insects, as well as religious books; all these show illustrations of people at work.

Generally speaking the people were greatly influenced by the Church, and most of them had complete faith; the

Church was part of their daily life; pictorial representation on the whole is grave and thoughtful.

The Crusades, later, had a great influence. The country was divided into small estates, each manor with its lord, its freemen, and serfs; the dependents of each manor regarding others almost as if they were foreigners.

The feudal system stands roughly for castles, open halls, and rather public living. There are many pictures of banquets, which are a great assistance in showing us small points of etiquette.

Some of the customs are of particular interest from the dramatic point of view. For example:

In Norman times the *mantle* was very important; boys would not be allowed to wear the mantle as it symbolized manhood.

To throw a mantle was a challenge.

In presenting a petition, the petitioner knelt and touched the mantle of the overlord.

A newly created knight was presented with a rich mantle by the sovereign.

If a messenger brought good news, he might be presented with the mantle then being worn by the receiver of the news.

Troubadours who pleased by their singing were similarly rewarded.

Norman scenes should be dignified and slow because of the clothes. The wearing of the mantle meant that a typical attitude had to be one hand on the hip, holding the mantle away from the body, preventing it from impeding the movement.

In Henry II's reign the male courtiers needed easier clothes to fit themselves to compete with Henry's energy and constant moving round his possessions. On occasions they hardly had time to sit down, even to eat, as no one could sit in his presence until he was himself seated.

There was more etiquette at this time than most people imagine.

It was the practice to eat with the fingers, but it was stated:

Hands should be clean.

Only three fingers to be used for helping oneself, the others to be gracefully extended.

The mouth should be wiped before drinking.

Ladies must not cram their mouths too full, or try to deprive their neighbours at table of the choicest bits.

In the twelfth century gloves took on the significance held by the mantle in the previous period.

To throw down a glove was now a challenge to mortal combat.

To give a messenger a glove was a sign of authority.

The right glove was always removed before greeting a friend or addressing a superior.

It was irreverent to enter a church without removing gloves.

Poisoned gloves were sometimes given.

The sleeve, too, held an important place:

Ladies liked to bestow them as love-tokens on their knights. Sometimes even a whole garment was given, which the knight would wear over his armour at the tournament, and come back with it gashed and rent, showing the rents with pride.

Sleeves were often detachable; it was a custom in the

tenth century for a queen to bestow her stylish sleeves on the poor.

In the fifteenth century we read of a costly sleeve being stolen from her arm, while a queen sat watching a miracle play.

A man would move freely, probably carrying one or both hands in his belt, his legs (when not covered by a cloak or robe) would be particularly noticeable because of the long tights; there would be no turn-out in the leg movement, and the feet would be parallel.

When he bowed he would slide one foot back leaving the weight on the front foot, both knees bent, the back heel off the ground, and again no turn-out. His body would tilt forward slightly as he removed his hat and brought it down to his side. He would then bring the foot forward again and replace his hat.

A lady's movement would be affected by her closely moulded gown with its very long voluminous skirt, often with a train and coloured under-skirt, so that she would find many ways of lifting her skirt for practical reasons, and always we see her holding it in decorative positions, also showing her hands to advantage, her body tilting back slightly as she walks. A widely varied range of elaborate head-dresses were worn.

In the later part of the period the mantle became a significant part of the woman's attire, because it was only worn by married women.

When the lady curtsied she would slide one foot back, dropping down on to the back heel, with her head up, and her hands by her sides; on rising, the back foot would come forward to the front one. The essence of the movement would be simplicity.

There are some stories about the women and their

clothes, which might well be developed into mime plays:

One story is about the women's trains:

That a woman with a long train passed by two monks; one monk saw a devil sitting on her train, and when she turned to the monk the devil fell off into the mud. Therefore we know that the devil hath power over women's long tails!

Another is about the elaborate head-dresses:

A famous monk travelled from place to place, preaching against these head-dresses, often collecting a congregation of 20,000 people (men one side, women the other),—the women 'like a forest of cedars with their heads reaching to the clouds'. He succeeded so well that 'many of the women threw down their head-dresses in the middle of his sermon and made a bonfire of them within sight of the pulpit'. For a time the monstrous ornament was pelted down by the rabble and stones were flung when people wore it. But the effect did not last long, and it is said that—'the women that, like snails in a fright, had drawn in their horns, shot them out again as soon as the danger was over'.

This, I am sure, brings to mind a number of interesting scenes for the classes to act, and in doing so, become accustomed to movement suited to mediaeval clothes.

It may be helpful to them to know a few more points of *etiquette of the early fifteenth century*.

If a gift was to be presented at a shrine, the hat was either held, or removed and placed on the ground beside the wearer, who knelt on both knees.

If a gift was to be presented to a human personage, the hat procedure was the same, but the giver knelt on one knee only.

If approaching a noble, the hat would be taken off, and the wearer fall on the right knee two or even three times, not replacing the hat until told to do so.

If two men met and greeted each other, each pushed off his

hat, so that it fell behind his shoulder. (This was the period when the liripipe was attached by a brooch.) The two men clasped right hands, but did not 'shake' them.

On entering the house it was customary to remove hood or hat, and gloves.

The lady knelt to God and high dignitaries on both knees. She often sat on the floor.

Two extracts from Books of Courtesy of the fifteenth century will assist in making scenes or plays:

The first one might make a children's scene.

'A schoolboy must bring pen, ink and paper with him, and on the way politely take off his cap to those he meets and give way to them on the road. At school, he should salute his master and the scholars, go straight to his place, undo his satchel and begin his lessons. He must work hard at his books if he wishes to be thought worthy to serve the State.'

The second gives a lovely banqueting scene:

'When you come to a feast, greet the steward who shows you where to sit—you will find bread laid for you and perhaps a platter also for soft food. There will be drinking cups upon the board and a salt cellar, but bring your own knife and spoon, the best you can afford.

When the food is brought around you will be served on to your trencher of bread or platter.

Eat quietly, and, as you share plates and cups do not leave your spoon in the food—or drink with your mouth full—lest you soil the cup.

Don't stroke the dog or cat under the table but keep your hands clean. Don't blow upon your food—but talk awhile pleasantly to your waiting friends while it cools. Don't put your elbows on the table or turn your back on your neighbour—do not inconvenience your host by calling for unserved dishes. Be sedate and courteous if you sit among gentlefolk—and tell no tale that would harm or shame any guest that so the feast may be pleasant to all.'

Perhaps one more extract may add flavour to the scenes. This is a foreigner's opinion of English people of the time; only helpful for senior or adult classes:

'The English are for the most part, both men and women of all ages, handsome and well-proportioned . . . great lovers of themselves and of everything belonging to them; they think that there are no other men than themselves, and no other world but England. . . . They all from time immemorial wear very fine clothes, and are extremely polite in their language. . . .

In addition to their civil speeches, they have the incredible courtesy of remaining with their heads uncovered with an admirable grace, whilst they talk to each other.

They are gifted with good understandings, and are very quick at everything they apply their minds to. . . . I have never noticed anyone, either at Court or amongst the lower orders, to be in love; whence one must necessarily conclude, either that the English are the most discreet lovers in the world, or that they are incapable of love.'

With some background of information from the teacher, the classes will certainly be able to develop scenes on the themes already given; on ladies and gentlemen banqueting in their great halls; troubadours bringing their songs and tales of love and war; or a romance between the troubadour and the young princess who may not realize her dreams; of gentlemen hawking, ladies on their way to Church, meeting one another; or ladies at home embroidering their tapestries, and receiving news or arrivals from the Crusades.

TUDOR PERIOD
End of fifteenth and whole of sixteenth centuries

To learn about the people of this period and the clothes they wore, we can still turn to sculpture and all forms of effigy, also to brasses and tapestries, and illustrated manuscripts which are often very beautiful; by now wood-cuts and metal-cuts, too, are a valuable source. We can look to the portrait painters—Memling, Dürer, Botticelli, Leonardo da Vinci, Titian, Holbein, and Raphael and, later in the period, at El Greco, and Rubens. There was at this time in England a spirit of enquiry and adventure, and more interest in travel; as a result there was less feeling of serenity than in the earlier periods, and the fashions of France, Holland, and Italy influenced England very much. As a result there was more breadth of outlook, and buoyancy of spirit, more learning, and more mental equality between the sexes, although Luther said:

'When women are ready in speaking it is not to be commended—there is no gown or garment that worse becomes a woman than when she will be wise.'

The girls' education was still deplorably low at the beginning of the period, but improved as time went on and Queen Elizabeth came to the throne.

The farthingale brought with it the fashion of sitting on a pile of cushions on the floor or on a joint stool; but towards the end of the century, specially made wide chairs were introduced, to accommodate the farthingale, though cushions were still quite popular.

Boys still waited at table, and a book on elegant deportment says:

'Boys of gentle birth when waiting at table must not scratch their heads or any other part of their persons, nor must they sneeze or cough into the dishes or drinking utensils.'

and again:

'Princely establishments must be conducted on different lines from common pothouses—all tin and pewter utensils to be scoured every Saturday, or at even shorter intervals if company was expected.'

There seems to have been a complete lack of cleanliness and hygiene from the sixteenth century; for public baths, which had been available in the fifteenth century, were then closed down as being breeding places for epidemics.

Outwardly, there was much luxury and pomp, and much use of perfumes, often in ball form, called pomanders.

Queen Elizabeth sent for a Flemish woman—Mistress Dingham Van der Plasse—who knew the secret of starch, and this lady earned great wealth giving lessons on ruff making and the secret of starch.

There was a story that amused Queen Elizabeth that might be made into a macabre mime:

'A lady of Antwerp who was in a great state because she could not get her ruff to set aright, in a passion called upon "the devil to take it". A handsome gentleman appeared. Together they tried to set the ruff; the gentleman strangled the lady and vanished. When they came to carry away the coffin no one could lift it, and when they opened it they found—a great black cat setting a ruff!'

In this period:

The man would walk easily, though his waisted tunic made his poise a little stiffer, and his feet were more turned out. Often he carried one hand on sword or belt, and before giving his hand to a lady he would kiss it. He also adopted the charming habit (probably French in origin) of kissing any article before handing it to a lady.

In *his bow* he would slide the right foot back, transferring his weight on to the back leg and bending the back knee. The front knee would be kept straight, and the body bowed. His hat would come down to the side with a curved arm position.

The lady's movement would be affected by the heavy materials of her dress, velvet, brocade, etc., often covered with quite weighty jewels. The wearing of the ruff or starched collar would encourage a well-poised head, and it was not considered correct for the farthingale to sway too much—so she would 'sail' as she moved, her hands on farthingale or stomacher.

Her curtsy would be much like the mediaeval curtsy, but looked very different because of the difference of timing: a quick drop and a slow rise; the hands on the skirt at either side at the beginning and coming up to cover the low-cut top of the dress on the downward drop.

Let the class now develop scenes for these times. Some of the most well-known happen to be the most dramatic:

Queen Elizabeth signing the death warrant for the Earl of Essex, *or*

Sir Francis Drake finishing his game of bowls as the Armada approaches.

The children will have plenty of suggestions of scenes about people in this period that they would like to act, and

K

will grow gradually more accustomed to moving as if wearing the clothes shown in pictures.

THE SEVENTEENTH CENTURY

Again it will be necessary to make a study of the costumes, and consider how they would affect the movements of the people who lived at this time. There are now many pictures available, and Van Dyck gives us an exact knowledge of the costumes that were worn. For a description in words, look at the pastoral called 'Rhodon and Iris', first acted in 1631, which contains a long and curious speech about the ladies of extreme fashion; or in Massinger's 'City Madam', the passage about a merchant's wife.

An interesting touch is that ruffs went abruptly out of fashion, because a physician's wife—condemned for her part in a poisoning case—went to her execution in a ruff; so they became unpopular.

Charles I had ideas about cleanliness that were ahead of his time, and he regarded fresh linen as being of great importance.

A book of rules in 1640 says:

'An occasional bath should be taken, the hands washed daily, and the face every day or so.'

A book of rules in 1624 refers to table manners in this way:

'Gentlemen to come sober and decently dressed to table, to refrain from sucking their fingers, using the table-cloth as a handkerchief, spitting into plates, throwing nibbled bones and crockery at each other, or "absent-mindedly" slipping their napkins into their pockets.'

In movement this was a rather pompous and affected period; dancing was much taught, and the 'turned out' line of the ballet was so much in vogue that it was said of Charles I that he 'walked as if he were dancing a measure'.

Deportment was learnt from these dancing-masters, including the use of the fan, and how to talk with it. There was a continental influence, and the women were treated like pretty dolls and in no way the marital equal of man.

'Bucket boots' were fashionable for a short time; the most extreme were as wide as a yard round the top, and tracts and pamphlets were written about the useless flapping tops of the rich:

'wasted leather that would serve the bare-foot poor'

which they said required their wearers

'to swagger like a bandy-legged duck'.

So this fashion did not remain long, but undoubtedly had some effect on the walk.

The Cavalier man would walk with a very turned-out hip line, almost doing a circular ballet movement on the ground with each step, his shoulders swinging in the open line with his foot, giving a swagger. In bowing he would sweep his hat off with a flourish, and hold it under his other arm, extending one foot forward, bending the back knee and tilting forwards, the empty hand remaining at his side. He would then take the hat again and replace it as he stepped forward to complete the movement.

The Puritan man had a much straighter line, and, of course, less swagger. His bow was much less elaborate; the step and inclination of the body being less, and the hat held with both hands in front.

The Cavalier lady would walk in the same way as the man, her full skirt (slashed down the front and looped up at the sides) swaying as she walked, and her bold eyes 'inviting'.

The Puritan lady would sway less as she walked, and her eyes would be downcast.

The Cavalier curtsy would be a step to one side, a closure of the feet, then bending both knees, she would look round at everyone in the room, as she dropped and rose again.

The Puritan curtsy would not be so deep, and would be more modestly carried out.

There are again plenty of opportunities for development of scenes based on this period:

—Cavaliers and Roundheads waiting for the Post to gallop into the village and bring news of the Civil War.

or

—Nell Gwyn—the orange girl—meeting Charles II.

A few other points of interest that might give background or suggestion for scenes are that:

—fish oil was used to make soap, and special soap was often made at home; seventeenth-century people washed in their own rooms.

Pepys, in his diary, says:

'My wife busy in going with her woman to the hot-house to bathe herself after her long being indoors in the dirt, so that she now pretends to a resolution of being hereafter very clean. How long it will hold I can guess.'

Then with regard to food, he says:

'Home from my office to my lord's lodgings, where my wife had got ready a very fine dinner, viz: a dish of marrow bones, a leg of mutton; a loin of veal; a dish of fowl; three pullets, and a dozen of larks all in a dish; a neat's tongue. A dish of anchovies; a dish of prawns and cheese.'

Coffee and chocolate had come into fashion, and doctors discoursed on the good and bad effects. To coffee they imputed moral effects, to chocolate the reverse!

Tea was also new enough for controversy. Amusing mime scenes could surely evolve round these discoveries.

THE EIGHTEENTH CENTURY

As in every period, some reading is necessary to feel the life of the time before thinking of the movement; and there are many authentic pictures of this period which can be of great assistance.

Dancing masters were even more famous than before. Everyone in society would learn to dance; all were slaves to rules of deportment, poise and elegance were of real importance; a man who wore the wrong kind of wig, or who behaved in an unfashionable way would immediately be an outcast from society.

A superficial wit was almost a necessity, as we see in the plays of Congreve and Sheridan. This is the peak of artificiality and of external effects. Underneath all the outward show of perfume and beauty, there was an incredible amount of dirt. Snuff was used, but not as often as is commonly supposed.

The man would carry his head well, and walk with his foot well turned-out, 'making a leg' showing his calf and red heel. His shoulders would be erect, chest well out showing his beautiful coloured silk waistcoat. His hands would be held gracefully, sometimes one on the hip, one perhaps carrying a handkerchief; the hand would never be on the sword unless to provoke a quarrel; if this happened even by accident, there would be a duel rather than a confession of a breach of etiquette.

To bow, he would remove his hat, placing it under the opposite arm and releasing the hand as in the seventeenth century. He would slide one leg forward—neatly turned out—then step forward closing the feet and replacing the hat. Sometimes the hat would be held in the hand with a good arm line. The hat was never placed on the heart.

The lady walked with the same feeling as the man, and of

necessity she had to carry her head well because of the size of her wig; at the height of the period the wigs were colossal erections covered with lace, ribbons, flowers, jewels, and all sorts of ornaments; the width of the skirt meant that the hands and arms were considerably used; they could not naturally fall at the side, and fans were greatly used and had significance.

The curtsy was much like that of the seventeenth century, with more ballet curve in the arm positions and some use of the fan while curtsying.

This period lends itself to many mime scenes:

An amusing scene would be of a dancing master and his pupils, watched perhaps by dowager parents who register their disapproval when necessary. The dancing master might perhaps invite his favourite pupil to remain behind.

A very different, but equally suitable subject might be that of:

The aristocrats being taken from their great houses to the guillotine in the French Revolution.

REGENCY OR EMPIRE

In 1810 when the mental state of George III made him unfit to rule—George—Prince of Wales became Regent. He was much more interested in dress than in affairs of state, and preferred the company of Beau Brummell to the company of his ministers. The word 'dandy' (applied to Beau Brummell) was first used at this period.

Looking at pictures of the time reveals what an amazingly sudden change in costume has taken place. At the end of the eighteenth century people had grown so tired of all the rules of deportment, that bows and curtsies disappeared and they began to use the hand-shake. The leg-line which had developed from being straight forward in the mediaeval times to being completely turned out in the eighteenth century, diminished, and a natural simplicity returned, with classical draperies, very flimsy at first, later becoming more substantial.

The man, influenced by a long era of warfare, walked with an upright bearing, using his legs well, conscious of his very tightly-fitting trousers.

In the bow he would push one foot slightly forward, bending the back knee, inclining a little forward.

The lady now walked with her arms at her sides, sometimes holding her skirt, using small steps, and occasional little runs.

The curtsy was not used so often, as shaking hands had become fashionable, and often the women kissed on both cheeks. If they curtsied, one foot would slide forward, the back knee bending, and as they stepped forward from it there would be a very slight waggle of the hips.

Appropriate mime scenes are again easy to find, based perhaps on the lives of Napoleon and Josephine, or of more simple folk—ladies sitting at home bored and dull, waiting for romance, while their young men are at the wars; then the excitement and intrigue among them when they go to the balls.

EARLY AND LATE VICTORIAN

As we move nearer to our own time, pictures become less necessary, family portraits and photographs, old-fashioned books and advertisements, can help us considerably, but it is important that the same respect be given to them; there always seems to be a tendency to burlesque this period.

Queen Victoria's influence effected a diguise of the natural line of the figure, feelings were hidden, modesty was predominant, and the back-board was the order of the day.

The influence of the Industrial Revolution seems to have been felt in the clothes also, and the men looked rather like black chimney-pots.

The mid-Victorian man was stiff (he wore corsets) and pompous, very conscious of his dignity as 'the head of the household'.

The bow—when used—was over the hat, which was placed in the middle of the chest, but shaking hands was common also.

The mid-Victorian lady was taught to cast her eyes on the ground and look demure, but her poke-bonnet would affect the way she looked about her, and indeed often encouraged a rather coy expression as she peeped out of it. As the crinoline was not allowed to bounce, she had to take very small steps, and her hands were often resting on it. It was a matter of art:

> to sit without steel hoops getting out of place
> to step into a carriage without crushing the tulle
> to travel
> to lie down
> to play with children

and it gradually went out of fashion for a man to offer his arm to a woman when accompanying her.

Handkerchiefs were always carried in the ladies' hands;— and it was said that 'the character of a woman could be ascertained by the way she held her handkerchief'.

The curtsy—when used—was a little bob inside the crinoline, one foot just behind the other.

The late Victorian man had a more debonair appearance, being no longer corseted as his father was. His cane gave him an air, his hat swept on and off as he passed by.

The late Victorian lady made the most of chest and bustle, and had a rather hollow-backed appearance. The wearing of a little 'pork-pie' hat perched on a mountain of hair, gave her a rather 'inviting' expression. She would shake hands rather high in the air, and her curtsy would be reserved for Court.

It would be good practice and amusing to mime two scenes—say in Hyde Park—one in early and one in late Victorian times.

The dramatic incident of the young Queen being shot at might be used for the first scene.

The second might be a domestic incident between two nursemaids with their perambulators (commonly seen in those days), quarrelling about the attentions of a passing soldier.

The history lesson may not gain very much from acting scenes from modern times, but classes will no doubt be interested to mime them and compare the difference of movement. The fact that there are such marked differences in the last hundred years makes it obvious that my earlier remarks covering whole centuries are only very broad generalizations.[1]

Here are some additional scenes which have dramatic incident and are likely to prove popular:

INFANTS

King Alfred burns the cakes.
King Canute tries to command the waves.
King Bruce and the spider.

JUNIORS

Romulus and Remus each decide to build a wall. Remus scoffs at Romulus' attempt and jumps the wall. Romulus kills him as he jumps.

[1] Excellent pictures illustrating costumes and customs of the different periods can be found in the following books which will be of great assistance to the classes: *Modes and Manners* by Max Von Boehm. (Translated by Joan Joshua, published by Batsford.) *The Life and Work of the People of England* by Hartley and Elliott. (Published by Batsford.)

With the help of these books, and the lead given in the notes above, some fresh and authentic work could be done.

Saint Joan leading her French troops.

Robin Hood, surrounded by his followers, Friar Tuck, Little John, Much etc., competes in an archery test and wins. As he is presented with the silver arrow he is recognized and taken prisoner. His followers help him to escape. King John and his yeomen and sheriff are left raging.

Florence Nightingale nursing in the Crimean War.

SENIORS

The murder of Thomas à Beckett.

Ann Boleyn hears news of her impending execution.

Christians in prison waiting to be thrown to the lions.

Old hags knitting, and watching the heads of aristocrats fall at the guillotine.

ADULTS

Hecuba hears of the fall of Troy, of the captivity of herself and her daughter.

Marie Antoinette saying good-bye to her son.

The Pump Room, Bath, 1720. Ladies and gentlemen meet to take the waters. The Duchess of Queensbury arrives wearing an apron costing 200 guineas after the fashion of the German woman. Beau Nash arrives, tears off the apron in disgust. She leaves in dudgeon.

*

Some knowledge and practice of historic movements are necessary before performing any period play, or the characters will look like people of today in fancy dress. For anyone who is hoping to make the theatre his career, considerable experience in this subject is essential.

XI

MASKS AND TRADITIONAL MIME

With classes of almost any age it is a useful experiment at some time to find out to what extent expression comes through the use of the body, and to what extent it is dependent on facial expression only.

As a test, ask the class to hang a handkerchief or scarf over their heads, letting it fall so that their faces are obscured. (The material must be sufficiently transparent for the actor himself to see where he is going.)

Suggest certain feelings to be shown in mime:

e.g. sorrow, fear, anger, happiness.

You will probably be surprised to find how little emotion is shown. The group will need to be convinced of this and will probably say that they were feeling deeply.

Let them repeat the exercise half at a time with the others watching; almost invariably the watchers will be amazed to see that although the groups were feeling so strongly, the expression had been largely confined to the face and that when this was covered the body described nothing. Once they have grasped this fully, they will soon improve.

Now ask the class to repeat the exercise realizing that the whole of the body must, as it were, take the responsibility. The movement and the expressive power of every part of the body will increase and strengthen through this practice, and it is quite a good plan to revert to it from time to time as a reminder.

I would do the exercise described above before starting any work in masks.

Infants and juniors are not so likely to do plays in masks as the seniors and adults, but the practice is still useful to the younger ones, for, apart from helping them to realize how much the body is capable of showing, the wearing of a mask gives a chance for the shy child to hide behind it and become someone else—like a puppet. This sometimes gives good results, and has a very good effect on the child.

Seniors and adults will become very interested in the different technique that is required for working in a mask.

It will be found that a good mask, or half mask, can be, and should always be, a work of beauty in itself, and when worn, the light will fall on it in so many ways, that it appears to take on different expressions. To make the most of this all the movement must be bigger than normal, it must be slower and more prolonged and there must be striking and often arrested positions. The gestures need to be wider— often with straight arms and legs, moving in big sweeps. A small movement of the head which would be quite effective without the mask would not show at all when masked, and a great deal of neck movement is needed to convey that the masked head is looking down or up or to the side: what may feel an exaggeration will probably be just right.

Most serious students of mime find this work absorbingly interesting, and love to watch one another and delight in the strange effects.

For some of them it will help if they are given a character

mask, and asked to wear it at every possible opportunity for a week, and then come back having developed the whole movement and character to fit the mask.

The same can be done with animal masks if they are to be used in a play, so that the actor, the character, and the mask grow together, and become one.

Four Plays for Dancers by W. B. Yeats are written specifically to be played in masks. They are most beautiful, and students will always be thrilled and excited by them; but they require experienced and expert speakers and movers. In these plays the technique I have just been describing could reach its culmination and fulfilment.

Some Characters of the Commedia dell' Arte

Students who are training for the theatre will no doubt be interested in studying the history of mime and will read widely to do so. An important part of that study will include the impromptu acting that was at its height in Italy in the sixteenth and seventeenth centuries.

This style of acting was known as the Commedia dell' Arte, and was a revival of the ancient Latin mimes who first performed comedies in Rome; they, in turn, were derived from the satirical buffoonery of the Greek comedies. Mime evidently provided a language that could be understood and appreciated by many nationalities and so had a universal appeal to all audiences; this was a great advantage with the widely varying peoples of the Roman Empire.

In the sixteenth century Ruzzante presented some comedies in which many parts of Italy were represented, each with its own dialect; from this, certain character types developed, and were acted all over Italy and France; some of these are still popular today, and should certainly be practised by adult students of mime, though they would have very little significance or value for children or in average classroom work.[1] Here, I will only attempt to outline the more obvious features of the major characters, and the way in which the companies worked.

The Commedia dell' Arte actors must have been highly skilled for they memorized no parts and acted impromptu. They were given the outline of a story, which was usually nailed up in the wings; the rest was invention. The good actor had to be capable of using his imagination, of reacting quickly and spontaneously to a given situation, and able to support his fellow players so that it all appeared to be rehearsed and prearranged. No amateur could hope to succeed in such conditions. Sometimes actors would change parts, and the same audience come again and again to enjoy the ingenuity and variety of the performances. Most of the actors were skilled in movement and even acrobatics, and descriptions of the plays of the time often include dancing, interpretation of animal movements, and mime as we know it, as well as improvised spoken scenes.

In our improvisation nowadays we are not really creating anything new, but are simply trying to renew an art that was very beautifully developed three or four hundred years ago.

The notes that now follow about some of the characters do not set out to be in any way a complete description, but— as those in the chapter dealing with historic movement—they hope to provide a lead which may encourage further study.

HARLEQUIN

As with all these characters, both the costume and behaviour of Harlequin have changed with the various actors who have played the part. He was originally just a lackey in tattered garments, using his wits to make a living. Many changes

[1] Those who intend to make a comprehensive study of this branch of work should read, *The History of the Harlequinade* by Maurice Sand.

took place, but it was the acting of Domenico that made Harlequin into the attractive character he has become. He is now recognizable by his many coloured diamond or lozenge-shaped spangles which cover his skin-tight garment, also by his black skull cap, his half-mask, and his baton which has magic powers. Harlequin is insolent, lively, and confident; popular with women, always successful in love, but often fickle. His mood changes like quick-silver; one moment he is petulant and childish, the next he is full of wit and he has flashes of brilliance; often he is a romantic lover with great personal magnetism. Sometimes he is in great poverty and difficulty, but he usually finds a way out for himself quite readily. He is essentially an acrobat and a dancer, amusingly supple and lively; his capers make him seem to be as much in the air as he is on the ground. Always he has an irresistible charm.

PIERROT

Pierrot also was at first a stupid lackey, who suffered from beatings and other indignities which made his audiences laugh; he was, in fact, originally a clown, but he became transformed by the acting of Deburau.

Like Harlequin, Pierrot can be petulant and childish, or a gay confident boy; but more often now we think of him as the poetical and romantic lover, usually dressed in white, or in pale sad colours. His completely white face and his black skull cap heighten his artistic and expressive powers. He is often the rival of Harlequin, but not often successful in love; at his moment of triumph, his loved one is usually lured away by someone else. More often than not, both are in love with Columbine, and while Pierrot is lost in a dream of the poetry that he may write to her, the more buoyant and confident Harlequin will whisk her away, and Pierrot is left more sorrowful and romantic than ever. His eyes stand out sadly in his mask-like face, and the lively supple dancing movements and beautiful vivid gestures seem to collapse in a moment, until he looks like a heap of garments on the floor, surmounted only by his black skull cap.

COLUMBINE

The nature of Columbine's part has varied with the many actresses who have played her, but certain characteristics are always recognizable. She is essentially a dancer, she is always young and attractive, usually very well aware of her charms and very ready to flirt. She would never hesitate to cast aside a former lover if she found another who would provide her with more wealth and luxury. She is fickle, and her fondness for ribbons, jewels, finery, will nearly always win her, and she will betray her master, or her lover, for these.

She may love Pierrot and Harlequin both at the same time, choosing first one and then the other to flirt with; she finds it fun to 'play-off' one against the other. Sometimes Columbine is the daughter of Pantaloon; she may be a heroine, or a waiting-maid, but whatever her part, she is still a dancer and a coquette, and she always wears a little apron by which we know her.

CLOWN

Clown is known to all, though we may still see him in many guises. He can usually be recognized by his traditional black wig with its long queue, his black corkscrew eyebrows, and his white cheeks with their cart-wheel of red and his large red mouth. Nowadays he frequently carries a string of sausages and lives in fear of the Police Constable.

Clown invokes laughter wherever he goes by his mistakes, his stupidity, or his tumbling. He possesses nothing, so may often play the part of a servant; he is always making jokes, and laughs more at his own jokes than at other people's.

Joe Grimaldi was the most famous of clowns of the eighteenth century, and he was much loved by his public. Another who has been greatly loved in our own time is Grock.

PANTALOON

Pantaloon is always an old man. Sometimes he plays the part of a doctor who may be clever and ingenious, but more often he creates trouble, or fun, by his lack of knowledge and the situations he causes. He is usually rather ridiculous in his desire to please, and is exploited by everyone. He is a good foil to Clown when they play together; Pantaloon himself is always duped, mocked, and unhappy. Sometimes he is represented as a father, and he is often an old miser.

His costume will vary with the part; but he will frequently be seen in a gaberdine and carpet slippers, with a woollen cap, and, of course, breeches and stockings all in one piece (pantaloons). Traditionally he has a grey moustache and beard, and very often a mask; sometimes he causes amusement by his knock-kneed gait, while Clown, in contrast, may walk with his knees turned out.

ISABELLA

In every comedy there must always be a beautiful heroine; no doubt there always has been. In 1578 Gelosi had in his troupe a leading lady whose name was Isabella; and ever since, the heroine in these plays has been Isabella. She is always exquisitely dressed, usually witty and vivacious, as well as being virtuous and beautiful. She is outstanding among women, and has real charm. Often Isabella will be the heroine with Columbine as her waiting-maid.

L

LELIO

Every play demands a hero as well as a heroine, and Lelio is this. He is always handsome, always immaculately dressed in the height of fashion, and nearly always favoured by parents because he is so rich and elegant. He usually plays suitor to the beautiful Isabella, although he may in some plays be in love with Columbine.

In the Italian comedies he is often maliciously placed in an awkward situation, for, although he looks so important and dignified and holds himself so proudly and stiffly, at the first sign of being caught in an intrigue or awkward situation not suited to his purpose he runs away! The hero humiliated in this way seems to have pleased the Italian sense of humour, and is far from our modern conception of a hero.

PULCHINELLA

Pulchinella is a character whose name has varied considerably with actor and period, and for years he was known as Polichinelle in the Italian troupes. In England he grew from Pulchinello through Punchinello to Punch. In France he was a famous marionette; and even as we know him now, both in our Punch and Judy show, and in our English magazine, we find many of his original characteristics:

He is ugly, he has a hooked nose and a hump; he laughs at life, but laughs with a certain cruelty. He carries a cudgel, and sometimes makes raucous cries like a bird of prey. He may look good-humoured, but underneath he enjoys a certain ferocity, and when you hear him laughing you should beware, for he has vicious qualities.

He has an easy conscience, and believes only in the futility of life's struggle, and objectively observes and takes advantage of humanity, amusing himself at the expense of others. He may play many roles, but his hunchback, and his coarse laughter will be present in whatever part he takes.

THE CAPTAIN

The Captain is always dressed with great grandeur; a hat with plumes, large moustache, a rapier at his side, a huge ruff, and brilliantly coloured doublet and hose. He is essentially a boaster, who struts about the world claiming credit for great feats that he has never performed.

At heart the Captain is a coward, but he boasts that there is nothing he cannot do; that women fall at his feet, that he can demolish a mountain as easily as fight a duel. Some people fear him, because they believe him, but many know that if he is attacked he will run away, and that he is all bravado, even though he looks as fierce as a tiger.

SCARAMOUCHE

Scaramouche is the son of the Captain, and he inherits some of his father's qualities, boasting of his conquests over women. Most of them instinctively fear him because of his sinister appearance—dressed in black from head to foot, with a very white face—but are captivated by his gifts of music and imaginative and enthralling talk. He plays a guitar, whiling away the time to cover up his intrigues of deceit and theft.

SCAPINO

Scapino is another intriguer, and another that has artistic gifts, for he is musical, he can sing, and he can dance; but he is much to be feared, and represents 'the mailed fist in the velvet glove'. He is ready to perform any service for money, takes on disguise easily and often he seems to be a trusted servant, but actually he is a clever thief and a liar. His costume varies but is frequently a rather showy livery of white, laced in green. He is dangerously attractive, and greatly favoured by young girls.

Lesser personalities

TARTAGLIA

The stutterer, always in a state of exasperation because he cannot complete his words, a figure of fun, accentuated even more by his enormous spectacles.

COVIELLO

A simpleton, famous for his grimaces, though he sometimes is played as a wit.

THE POLICE CONSTABLE

In various guises he was always part of the Italian comedy, representing justice.

THE CANTATRICE

She was used as a pretty singer to fill in any interval and keep the continuity of the performance.

THE BALLERINA

She would dance during intervals in the performance. Both singer and dancer might be asked to fill other roles such as Isabella or Columbine—but, as in the theatre nowadays, the size of the company depended on circumstances.

There are countless other characters not mentioned here and there is much more to learn about them all, and anyone who wishes to become a serious student of mime should study this history in greater detail and treat these notes only as a beginning. It is interesting to realize that these characters are really applicable to every play and to every age:

the hero, the heroine, the successful and unsuccessful lovers, the mistress, the maid, the old gentleman and the servant, the maker of fun, the braggart, the evil-doer;—none of them is new to us, but the style of acting in the sixteenth and seventeenth centuries was particular to the Italians of that time.

Any senior schoolchild, or any advanced student, might find it of value to use these notes about the characters and to go through the process I described earlier, of concentrating and thinking himself slowly into a character, to see if he can bring to life in the same way these characters which were so vital a part of drama three hundred years ago.

Traditional Gestures

It is certain that there was a convention of gesture, and that it made a language significant to and understood by the audiences. We are indebted to Irene Mawer for her research and the revival of these speech gestures.[1]

There are charming gestures for:
'A lady', 'A gentleman', 'Money', 'No money', 'Exquisite', 'A letter', 'Look over there', 'Hungry', 'Asleep', 'Hark', 'Listen', 'Will you marry me'—and others.

These are only suitable for use in a traditional mime play —for example, one in which the traditional characters of the Commedia dell' Arte appear, or possibly in certain period plays of a rather stylized kind. They are *quite unsuitable and out of place* in a modern mime play.

The gestures themselves are valuable practice for most ages (not infants) because they give a neatness and precision of movement that it does not seem possible to induce without this kind of practice. They are, however, so 'continental' in flavour that their style is not easy for the average

[1] In her book *The Art of Mime* Irene Mawer gives a full description of the speech gestures.

Britisher; but the very fact that they do present this difficulty makes them, I think, all the more useful as a practice.
Everyone seems to enjoy doing them, whatever the age, and
although there can be no logical reason for teaching them in
schools where mime plays of this particular kind are not
likely to be produced, yet, I would occasionally allow the
children to attempt them as a special treat—rather than a
regular routine—just because they are invariably so interested in knowing about them.

L'Enfant Prodigue

This chapter cannot end without some mention—however
brief—of the great three act mime play L'Enfant Prodigue.
The music is by Wormser, and every bar of it is interpreted
in the mime; the music and mime are one.[1]

The music is available, and the story is clearly written
above the musical line; but much detail is left to the individual interpretation of the artist; there is sometimes a page
or two of music to cover one simple instruction, such as—

'He writes,' or
'The reading of the letter.'

—it is necessary for producer and players to realize that every
bar of the music has dramatic significance and should be
used.

The play is only suitable to work with advanced students,
but they will certainly find it an exciting study and a great
experience.

[1] Irene Mawer speaks fully of the play in The Art of Mime.

XII

MUSIC AND MIME

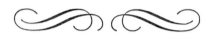

Any mime class can be helped very greatly by a good pianist, but unless he is a real musician and capable of improvisation of the right kind, it is usually wiser to do without music altogether. If he is not able to improvise it is certain that the speed and impetus of the class will suffer, and then little will be gained, unless possibly he is able to be of use for the rhythmic accompaniment which is always helpful for physical exercises.

To be of real use, the ideal mime pianist should himself know something about mime. This knowledge can of course grow, with the experience of playing for mime, but his thought has to be very concentrated, since he is really composing all the time. He needs to be able to imagine all the moods or characters the class are asked to convey, and to translate these into music; the music cannot be just expressive, but must also have the quality of the movement in it. Some pianists are able to improvise well, but are apt always to use one key, and fail to grasp the change of character or mood that is given by the change of key. If, for this, or any other reason, all their improvisations sound alike, the classes quickly lose vitality.

Few pianists, however good as performers, seem to have all the qualities that are needed for accompanying mime;

perhaps they really need all the instincts of both dancer and actress in addition to their musical abilities. Playing for mime classes needs much greater skill than playing for dancing classes, as there can be almost no routine, and the pianist must be entirely creative.[1]

I am often asked to give advice about pianists for mime, and I would say that a very great deal of mime can be entirely satisfactory without accompaniment, and the teacher will find that it is happier to be without a pianist than to have the wrong one!

The teacher can, however, decide either:

To use rhythmic accompaniment, such as drums, tambour, cymbals, bones, etc., or:

To learn enough about music himself to be able to describe briefly to an inexperienced pianist what his need is. He should be able at least to indicate time-signature and tempo of whatever he requires.

My hope is that *Music for Mime* will help to solve this difficulty for teachers.

Another important point to realize is that it is very bad for a class to become too dependent on the pianist and perpetually look to him for a lead; so it is all to the good that some of the work should be unsupported by music.

Certainly it is a great help to have accompaniment for physical practice, also for imaginative or abstract work that is dependent on a mood and atmosphere. Music also helps to cover the self-consciousness that sometimes grows in

[1] I have been very fortunate in having an ideal partner to play for my classes, and Barbara Lander in filling this role has made a great contribution to our work together. At my request, she has composed short pieces of music to accompany many of the expressive exercises in this book, and also music for some of the mime plays. We hope that it may be a help both to mime teachers and mime accompanists, as it gives them a starting ground, which may be a guide to improvisations of their own.

The music is published by Methuen & Co., Ltd., under the title of *Music for Mime*. This is also available on records produced by Discourses Ltd.

silence. The teacher will find himself talking much more, and building the atmosphere by means of speech, when he has no music; but for the main bulk of the simple practice demanded in this book music is not in any way essential, and most general teachers who introduce a little mime into their other classes will certainly not want or need music.

Animals, characters, occupations, improvisations, all these can be taught equally well, if not better, without any music at all. It is in traditional mime, and speech gesture leading to conventional mime plays that the need for music grows.

Much depends on the circumstances; if mime is going to be developed seriously as an art, accompaniment becomes an almost essential part of it. If it is a small part of other classroom work, or an addition to Speech and Drama classes, music would be quite unnecessary.

If mime is in any way linked up with music teaching in a school, the art of musical interpretation becomes important; this should not be confused with dance interpretation. A good mover can fairly easily interpret music at any rate to some extent in a dance form. It seems to need a different approach to interpret the music in dramatic form.

Mime is one of the most exciting subjects it is possible to teach, but it is also a subject which can fail completely if it is allowed to do so. It is so pitifully easy to go on teaching old material that has been successful. Although the classes may be fresh ones, the teacher himself loses vitality and interest unless the repetitions are renewed in spirit and brought to life again.

Remember too, that the young are living in advance of us and that we must keep abreast of life with them. If we believe that our work will contribute in any way to the betterment of man, we must strive to do it with inspiration.

XIII

MIME PLAYS

I have always found in working out mime plays that it is easier to produce a good result if the play is made especially for a particular group of people. I think many teachers find this to be the case, and so prefer to make their own. Some teachers may feel that they are not very inventive, but they need not be dismayed, for there are so many sources to which to turn for plot.

Think of all the stories there are in the world—great stories of all generations and all nations, legends, folk tales, fairy stories, stories from Greek mythology, Bible stories, poems, ballads, songs, operas—a supply without limit.

Select an episode or tale that is likely to be suitable for a mime play; which means that if possible it should be complete in one scene (although this is not a necessity). It should be pictorial, with dramatic incident that will bring it to a climax, without being too dependent on dialogue. I should perhaps mention that it is a legitimate and normal practice to print a brief synopsis in the programme when a mime play is being performed.

Those who have creative gifts will probably want to use their own plots and will not want to depend on other sources, but in either way good mime scenes and plays can develop.

This method pre-supposes that you will make your play and find your music afterwards; unless you are fortunate enough to have it composed for you as the play develops, which of course is ideal; but set accompaniment is essential; improvised music tends to lengthen each episode, and style is lost.

Some people, on the other hand, find that listening to music and allowing their imagination to roam is as profitable a source of inspiration as any.

As long as the final result is a good mime play, the method of creation matters very little. Here follow some suggestions of plays which I have evolved, tried out and proved to be successful. Most of these are free mime, and traditional gestures would in these be quite out of place; where they would be appropriate I have mentioned the fact. I have made notes about music or sound effects which will, I hope, be helpful. Barbara Lander has composed music for a number of the plays—this is included in the publication *Music for Mime*.[1] I shall be very happy if some of these plays are of use to other teachers and their classes.

[1] In order not to burden this book with details of every move in *Prometheus, The Wicked Piper, Ten Little Sailor Boys, The Young King* and *The Village Concert*, Barbara Lander has given directions above the appropriate phrases in her music.

PROMETHEUS

A mime play based on Greek mythology—with music composed by Barbara Lander. This is suitable for seniors or adults, but could be simplified for work with juniors.

Characters

Zeus (King of Heaven)
Ares (God of War)
Hera (Queen of Heaven)
Pallas Athena (Goddess of Wisdom)
Artemis (Goddess of the Chase)
Hephaestos (God of Fire)
Hermes (Messenger of the Gods)
Eros (Child God of Love)
Other Gods and Goddesses as numbers allow
Prometheus (who stole Fire from Heaven to benefit Mankind) ⎫
Epimetheus (Brother of Prometheus) ⎬ Both originally among the Gods
A Vulture ⎭
Hercules (the strongest among mankind)
Mankind (at least a dozen, preferably about twenty, according to space)

Costumes

The Gods should be dressed and made-up with great beauty, following for their pattern the finest statues and pictures.

The Vulture should be dressed to suggest the bird.

Mankind should look as wild and primitive as possible. Hessian tunics are quite effective, with bare limbs made up darker than usual, and unkempt hair.

Set and Lighting

The skycloth or cyclorama must be lit to represent the vault of heaven.

Up stage right there should be rostra of varying levels, up to about 6 feet if possible, so that we can open with a fine group of the Gods on Olympus. Zeus and Hera will be enthroned at the top, and the others decoratively grouped below them at different levels almost to the ground.

Down stage centre Mankind will be grouped on the ground, looking like a dark mass that might be mistaken for rock.

Up stage left there should be a rock-like formation on which Prometheus can stand when he is chained on the side of the mountain. He must be raised above Mankind, but not as high as Olympus.

At the opening the Gods must be in a flood of light, and Mankind and the mountain in shadow. As Eros comes to earth there should be a gradual increase of light on Mankind for the Creation—the Gods still being just visible—but not 'flooded'.

As the play proceeds, there should be alternating light on Mankind and the Gods for their particular scenes.

Hercules must of course be well lit for his battle with the Vulture, and there should be a 'spot' up stage left on the mountainside which can be brought on to Prometheus when he is being tortured by the Vulture.

The lighting of Mankind can vary to help the mood; for example, during the scene of war, Mankind can move in silhouette with a red glow behind, whereas in the scene of hunger a much colder light will be effective.

At the general rejoicing on the final curtain, everything should be brought 'full-up'.

Theme of the Play

The Gods are on Olympus feasting and content. Zeus

desires that there shall be life on earth, and sends Eros to earth to create life. Watched by the other Gods on Olympus, Eros floats down to earth and begins by creating plants, trees, birds, and animals; then pleased with his work he returns to Olympus, and all the Gods watch the earth with pleasure. Zeus is still not satisfied; therefore he sends Prometheus and his brother Epimetheus to mould man from clay. They make their way to earth, and from the dark mass of rock they weld man; he is made in the likeness of the Gods (the only model they have), but even though he is well-shaped, he is still rigid and without life. Eros is sent again from Olympus and floats among Mankind giving him breath, so that he begins to live and move. Still Zeus is not satisfied with his creation, so with great power and majesty Pallas Athena comes to imbue man with soul. Mankind sees the Gods, realizes he is created in their likeness, feels the moving spirit in his breath and soul, is over-awed and kneels in gratitude to the Gods.

Time has passed on the earth: Man must eat and drink, he looks around to find food and water. He is primitive, he is hungry, he grabs what he can get at, and eats ravenously. He feels cold, he shivers and huddles with others, instinctively knowing his needs. Only Prometheus, who has not returned to Olympus with the other Gods, is watching mankind closely. He sees their plight, and sees Hephaestos holding the torch of fire in Heaven; without further thought, he leaps towards the fire, snatches it and runs with it to Earth, where he stands holding out the flame happily, as Man clusters round taking pieces of fire away to serve his various needs. Man is grateful and warms himself contentedly. But Zeus is jealous and angry at this theft and gift, and as we turn back to Olympus we see him rise on his throne to punish. He orders Ares and Hephaestos to capture Prometheus and chain him to a rock on the mountainside. There for years he is to be tortured by a vulture who will devour his liver all day, and each night it will grow again while the Vulture sleeps. Prometheus is chained to the rock and left to his fate. Zeus commands the Vulture to attack and it does so.

Ares is now ordered by Zeus to punish Man also for taking Prometheus' gift. Unaware of the dissension between the Gods, Man is contentedly warming himself and cooking the food he has found. Ares goads one man to snatch food from another, a third to snatch fire, and quickly he has incited War; and fire that was to be man's comfort has become a weapon of War. All we can see now is primitive fighting; until, inevitably, War has exhausted the world, and Mankind lies panting and waiting for death; while the Vulture again visits Prometheus who is suffering for Mankind. Then from out of this heap of desolation the great hero Hercules arises; he sees Prometheus in torment, and watched by the Gods and all Mankind, he struggles with the Vulture just as it is about to approach Prometheus again. The conflict is terrifying, but finally Hercules kills the bird, climbs to Prometheus, releases him from his chains, and Hercules is welcomed by Zeus on Olympus as a great hero, and invited to drink of the nectar of the Gods; while Prometheus remains on earth beloved of mankind.

ABU-HASSAN

A mime play based on a story from *The Arabian Nights*. The comedy of this makes it suitable for Seniors and Adults; but Juniors would no doubt enjoy it and play it with a deadly seriousness, which might be quite successful, though I envisage it as light-hearted comedy or farce for more mature students.

Music

I would suggest melodies from well-known songs. Choose a different theme for the entrance and action of each character. This I think will heighten the fun, and can be arranged quite simply by a good accompanist—e.g. 'The Teddy Bears' Picnic' for the Creditors or 'The Temple Bells' (Indian Love Lyrics) for the Caliph's Ambassadors.

Characters

> Abu-Hassan
> His Wife—Fatima
> Kayah—their faithful Servant
> Omar—the Banker
> The Three Creditors
> The Caliph
> His two Ambassadors
> Wife of the Caliph
> Her two Ambassadors
> Attendants on the Caliph
> Attendants on the Caliph's Wife

If further characters are desirable, it is possible to follow the Caliph's procession into the house with a street crowd.

Costumes

Eastern flavour. Can be very simple—baggy trousers, wide

waist-bands and turbans for the men—veils, robes, etc., for the women.

Set and Lighting

The lighting for this can be very simple as it is an interior scene without need for variety. The time can be morning or afternoon; if a change of light is simple and desirable a window could be imagined right, and the brilliant afternoon sun throwing its beam across the room, could change as the sun sinks towards evening.

The room must be Eastern in style, though not wealthy; some cushions about the floor, a divan diagonally placed stage right, and a table with bowls of tea or iced drinks towards the left. A door down stage left leading to Fatima's bedroom, and double doors up stage centre which lead to the street; in these doors there should be a little flap or grill through which the servant can peep and give warning of the people who are approaching the door.

Theme of the Play

Abu-Hassan and his wife, Fatima, are at home happily together. Everything is not as happy as it would appear, however, as they are seriously in debt! Abu says to Fatima, "I have no money." Fatima says to Abu, "I have no money." Both together they say, "*We* have no money." Then they shrug their shoulders, pour themselves out a bowl of tea, sit down, stir it, smile at each other, drink the tea, and enjoy it. They move precisely together, as if they were of one mind in all they do or think. (This precision is essential to the light-hearted style of the play.) Suddenly, the big doors up stage centre open, and in comes Kayah, their trusted servant, shutting the doors quickly behind him. He agitatedly tells them that three creditors are on their way down the street coming to demand that their debts should be paid. Kayah looks several times through the grill announcing each

M

time that they are nearer than before. Abu says, "I will not see them." Fatima says, "I will not see them." Both say, "*You* must see them." There is a knock on the door, Abu and Fatima together say, "*We* are *out*." Fatima runs into her room, Abu hides behind the divan. Kayah opens the door, and there are the three creditors, one very tall, one of medium height, and one very small! They are all very solemn, and all move identically together. "We want our money," they cry. The servant protests that he cannot help, his master and mistress are out. "Nonsense," say the creditors and push their way in. Solemnly following one another (the tallest first, and the smallest last) they walk in a line about the room, peering into everything they can find in search of any money there may be. Abu is nearly caught several times, but avoids them by following round behind the last one, until they go out again the way they came in, angrier than before. Fatima has been listening and returns, and the three together discuss what is to be done.

Suddenly Abu has an idea. He and Fatima will each in turn pretend that the other is dead, then the Caliph will have to provide money for Fatima's funeral and the Caliph's wife will have to provide money for Abu's funeral. In this way, they will be able to pay their debts, and start life in another place. Fatima and the servant are in full agreement with the plan, and all is bustle and excitement. The servant is sent out to take a message to the Caliph that Fatima is dead, and Abu after instructing his wife to be prepared to appear to be dead, kisses her good-bye and follows after the servant to collect the money.

Fatima sets about preparing the room for the arrival of guests, when there is a knock at the door; she peeps through the grill, and to her surprise sees that it is Omar, the Banker. Rather reluctantly (for he is a renowned rogue) she lets him in, wondering why he has come. To her horror and astonishment he begs her to leave her husband and come away with him; Fatima refuses, but Omar promises that if she will come with him, he will settle all Abu's debts. Fatima begins to be frightened of his passion, so, pretending to agree, she persuades him to hide in the next room on the pretext that Abu will be returning. Duped by this, Omar willingly goes into her bedroom, and before he has time to turn round she has skilfully contrived to lock him in. At this moment Kayah returns saying that Ambassadors from the Caliph are close behind him on their way to establish that Fatima is dead. A moment later Abu returns; he is just in time to act the kneeling mourner over Fatima who is lying with folded hands on the floor, as the servant opens the door to the Ambassadors from the Caliph. Very pompously and with stylized extravagant movements they come to the centre moving precisely together; they observe the wailing mourner, the corpse and the miserable-looking servant. The first Ambassador lifts one arm of the corpse, the second lifts a leg; both remain stiffly and ridiculously in the air! The Ambassadors look at one another, tap the leg and arm, which fall suddenly to the ground; the Ambassadors look completely satisfied, hand two bags of money to Abu, and walk out in the same pompous way that they came in. Immediately they have gone, Fatima jumps up, and they all rejoice at the size of the money bags. Quickly the servant, Kayah, is sent out again, this time to the Caliph's wife to tell her that Abu has died, and to collect money for his burial. In the meantime, Abu prepares to put on an appearance of looking dead and teaches Fatima to act as mourner, and back comes the servant bringing two Ambassadors from the Caliph's wife to establish his death.

These two, belonging to a different household have a different set of movements but they are quite as stylized and peculiar as the other Ambassadors. To them, this is an everyday job and they have no interest greater than their own appearance, so they go through the same performance as the other two, give the money to Fatima, and depart. Now, of course, Abu is full of life again, overjoyed by the success of his plan and ready to be off, conveniently forgetting about his debts. But there is an ominous knock at the door. Kayah peeps out and reports that the creditors are again on the doorstep. Fatima remembers Omar, she cannot run to her room, together they crouch behind the divan with their bags of money, determined not to give it up now they have got it. Once again the creditors force entry, suspecting that money has come into the house, and once again, after trying to nose it out (and as before, only just missing Abu *and* Fatima by seconds) they depart disappointed.

Now all seems to be settled, and Abu and Fatima prepare to fly, when again there is a knock at the door. The servant now reports an unexpected turn of events; the Caliph and his wife are at the door together! Their suspicions have obviously been aroused by the two deaths, and they realize that they have been duped! What can be done now? Instantly, Abu has another idea, they can *both* be dead and the servant must turn mourner. Quickly Abu and Fatima lie with the soles of their feet touching and their hands clasped on their breasts. Kayah opens the door, and then runs weeping to his apparently dead master and mistress.

The Caliph and his wife are, of course accompanied by their retinue and their entrance is most impressive, still in the same stylized manner of the Ambassadors, but with even more ceremony. (They may be followed by a crowd from the street.)

Having expected to find they had been tricked, the Caliph and his wife are astonished to find that in fact both Abu and Fatima are dead; and the servant's grief is so real that no other investigation is necessary.

"Now," says the Caliph, "which of these two died first? One of them was due to receive money but not both. If Abu died first, you pay, if Fatima died first, I pay." There is consternation among the crowd, everyone substantiates a different theory, the servant is too grief-stricken to take any part; a quarrel develops between the Caliph and his wife, and the crowd stare bewildered as they argue. "She died first." "No, he died first." "No, *she* died." "*He* died." "SHE." "HE.", etc., rising to a crescendo of excitement as they speak (in mime, of course) more and more quickly, and then both together!

For a moment there is quiet, no one knows what to do next, then the Caliph makes the following announcement:

"I will pay 1,000 gold pieces to anyone who can give us a true and certain answer to this problem, and can tell us which of these two died first."

There is a buzz of excitement among the crowd; all of them would like to solve the riddle and earn the money, but now Abu again uses his wits, and much to everyone's astonishment, he jumps up, followed by Fatima, and apologizes to the Caliph and his wife, and claims the 1,000 gold pieces by confessing everything and so solving the problem. Fortunately for Abu, the Caliph enjoys the cleverness of the trickery and treats it as a joke, and after a solemn moral warning the Caliph gives Abu his 1,000 gold pieces. At this moment, there is a tremendous noise from the inner room, and Fatima explains her difficulties with Omar. Omar is disliked by everyone in the town, and her story is easily accepted; she now opens the door and he comes storming out in a great rage; he did not, however, expect to find the Caliph and his train, and is even more angry when the Caliph orders two of his attendants to remove Omar and punish him. The people of the town are fond of Abu and Fatima, so there is general rejoicing and amusement as the Caliph and his wife make their ceremonious exit in gayer mood than when they came in.

When the crowd has dispersed, Abu and Fatima sink contentedly on to the divan, and the servant pours them out a bowl of tea. They stir it, smile at one another, drink and enjoy the tea, just as they did at first—but their movement and mood of enjoyment is suddenly arrested when they hear from the servant (and *we* hear by the repeated theme in the music) that the creditors are once more approaching the house.

As the curtain falls we see Abu and Fatima gather up the bags of money they had received for the burials, and we know by their disconsolate faces that this time the creditors will be paid! But Abu gives us a knowing wink and hides away his 1,000 gold pieces just before we lose sight of him.

Notes. Whatever music is selected, the characters must be very obviously marked by change of theme and recurring theme, and the movement must be precise and clear on each beat. Traditional gestures would be quite suitable in this play, though not essential. With Seniors and Adults the miming of the mood with the music is half the fun. With Juniors it might be better to let them improvise with speech and use no music, unless they are especially skilled in mime.

THE WICKED PIPER

A mime play for Juniors with music composed by Barbara Lander. (Students might enjoy performing this also.)

Characters

A young peasant man
His wife
A wicked old piper
At least five elves (preferably ten or eleven)
At least four monsters (preferably seven or eight)

Set and Lighting

The scene is a clearing in the forest, a few trees and an old tree stump towards the left of the stage which serves as a seat. Up right of the stage is a grassy bank leading out and away into the distance. It is late afternoon, but the light fades from rather brilliant sun to twilight—so that there is a dim and misty effect when the old piper enters; by the time he goes out, the moon has risen, so that the ending is again in a flood of light, though of a different quality.

Costume

The peasants can be of any national costume provided it is in keeping with the set, or they can be dressed in simple English style. The elves in gay colours and the monsters predominantly green and brown, resembling evil spirits from the roots of the trees.

Theme of the Play

In a wood in early spring two little elves are playing; they run in and out of the trees playing hide-and-seek. Presently they tire of the game and sit together at the foot of a tree left, playing at cat's cradle with a length of gossamer thread. Two others come running down the grassy bank from up stage right, leap-frogging as they come; quickly they busy themselves scattering seeds and watching to see how quickly they will grow. Another elf comes from up stage left and looks round to see what mischief he can do; he is the naughtiest, and starts off by disturbing the two at cat's cradle—then he makes a nuisance of himself by teasing the other two each in turn in different ways.

The two playing cat's cradle tire of their game and set about making magic and willing the flowers to grow; all of them are busy and only disturbed by the mischievous elf, when suddenly they hear a sound. It is a weird piping, something they haven't heard before; they become frightened and huddle together, and as it comes nearer they run away to the right and hide in a thicket close by,—from time to time we see them peeping out, so we know that they are aware of all that is happening. The piping comes nearer, and from the left, coming from behind the trees, grotesque monsters appear, large and terrifying. They dance round in a circle and then turn and herald the entrance of an old piper; he is ugly and scowling, and the music that comes from his pipe is not beautiful but strange. The monsters dance again to his pipe, preparing evil magic, and the elves in their cover become more and more frightened.

Suddenly there is a stir among them, they have heard something which disturbs them, the piper makes a sign and quickly the monsters change themselves into trees, and the piper hides behind one of them—staring at the grassy bank up stage right. From the top of the bank we now see a happy young couple—a peasant and his wife—they have lost their way and are glad to find this clearing and a tree stump to sit on: the woman sits to rest, and the man gathers some flowers for her and comes and sits by her on the ground. Rested, they decide it is time to move on, especially as it is clear that darkness is coming fast; at this moment they are arrested by

the sound of piping, and the old piper emerges from behind
the tree coming closer and closer to them, as if bewitching
them with his music. The peasant woman is fascinated, gets
up and begins to follow the old piper, as if she hardly knew
why; her husband realizes what is happening and entreats
her not to follow, but she is spellbound and begins to dance
in and out of the trees following the piper as he threads his
way with malicious delight at the power he has over her.
Her husband tries to follow, but the monsters that were
trees come out and bar his way. He is fighting to get to his
wife, struggling and nearly at his wits' end, when the elves
boldly rush out of their cover and surround the piper; they
battle with him and wrench the pipe from his lips. Immediately the piper is forced to stop playing. Having lost his pipe,
his power is lost also and he is afraid; at the same moment
that the pipe is wrenched from him, the monsters recoil, as
if they too were powerless; the mischievous elf now finds a
use for his quick wits, and runs with the pipe to the young
peasant, pressing him to play it, for as yet his wife still
seems bewitched and in a dream. Immediately the young
man begins to play the most beautiful music issues from the
pipe; the old piper struggles to get near enough to the
peasant to regain his pipe and his power, but the music of
the pipe is now too strong for him, and gains power all the
time. The young man moves towards his wife, and the
monsters and the wicked piper, struggling to free themselves
from this new magic, run away on all sides looking uglier
than ever, and writhing in contortions as if they were in
pain. At the same time, the young wife is freed from her
enchantment and returns with joy and relief to her husband;
as he joins her he throws the pipe to the elves; they are
highly excited, and playing happy music on the magic pipe
they lead the couple safely away to show them their road
home.

TEN LITTLE SAILOR BOYS

A mime based on a nursery rhyme, with musical variations composed by Barbara Lander on a traditional tune.

This mime could be attempted by any age. Juniors will enjoy playing it quite freely without troubling about the accompaniment, probably adding their own noises. Seniors and Adults will find it more effective if they realize that unlike some of the other mimes which are rather free in expression, this one needs to be *drilled*. The fun is gained from the precision of the sailor boys' movement interpreting each note of the music, and their movements when in unison being exactly together. Expert timing and finish is necessary.

Characters

Story Teller

Ten Sailor Boys (they can be all one size, or ranging from very small to large—grouped in height—smallest first)

A Mermaid

A Bee

A Beehive (three or more people)

A Fish (two people)

A Big Bear

A Baby Bear

Two Penguins (some other animals if desired)

A Parson

A Bride

One little girl

Set and Lighting

No special scenery or lighting, but as much space as possible.

Costume

The Story Teller could be dressed as an old salt or sea captain. The other characters can wear a uniform basic garment (black or navy) and suggest the costume by slight additional accessories:

The Sailor Boys could wear white duck trousers, striped blue and white T-shirts with red neckerchiefs, and round shiny black hats with ribbons, and elastic under the chin, so that they can at times be pushed back and hang at the back of the neck. Feet would be bare.

A Mermaid should have long hair which she can comb, a beautiful tail attached from the waist which she can spread out as she sits.

A Bee—antennae on the head, and possibly wings would be quite sufficient.

A Beehive—the three or four people concerned will together with uplifted hands support the straw top to a hive, so that they appear to be the walls—their uniform will be sufficient.

A Fish could have a mask attached to the right side of one person's face and the left side of the other person's face. Both will be facing forward with one arm extended forward palm to palm and bodies close together. The shape of the fish face can be indicated in the mask, the eye in the side. A tail will be draped from the mask on each side and trail after them as they walk. The front arms will represent the jaw which will engulf and swallow the boy, who will then come between them.

The Two Bears—Fur gloves (with claws attached) and fur bonnets.

Two Penguins—Penguin half masks, possibly flappers.

A Parson—A curate's hat, coat, and collar.

A Bride—Orange blossom, veil and bouquet.

A Little Girl—A sunbonnet.

Make-up should be straight.

Theme of the Play

This is of course apparent from the words of the nursery rhyme, but there are a variety of versions of it. Below is the version used for this mime:

1. Ten little sailor boys
   Going out to dine
   One over-ate himself
   And then there were nine.

2. Nine little sailor boys
   Staying up late
   One over-slept himself
   And then there were eight.

3. Eight little sailor boys
   Going down to Devon
   One saw a mermaid
   And then there were seven.

4. Seven little sailor boys
   Chopping up sticks
   One chopped himself in half
   And then there were six.

5. Six little sailor boys
   Playing near a hive
   A big bee stung one
   And then there were five.

6. Five little sailor boys
   Studying the law
   One stayed in Chancery
   Then there were four.

7. Four little sailor boys
   Swimming in the sea
   A big fish swallowed one
   And then there were three.

8. Three little sailor boys
   Visiting the Zoo
   A big bear hugged one
   And then there were two.

9. Two little sailor boys
   Lying in the sun.
   One got frizzled up
   And then there was one.

10. One little sailor boy
    Left all alone
    He got married
    . . . . .

Note. The play opens with the entrance of the Story Teller, who saunters across and stands down left or right of the stage. He speaks with a dialect and introduces each episode by speaking the lines. He speaks one verse, then the music takes it up, never the two together. The action of the mime takes place between the speaking of each verse, the actors remain 'frozen' until the music begins.

All the extra characters (e.g. the Mermaid, the Bee, the Hive, the Fish, the Zoo, the Parson) remain on the stage after their part is finished as part of the tableau; so do the Sailor Boys after they have 'died'.

VERSE I

The ten Sailor Boys run on in single file and round the stage from up left in a semicircle to down right, and from there the leader goes again in a semi-circle up stage and round to down left, followed by the others, until he is opposite number ten who has by then arrived down stage right (see diagram). They sit exactly together, in a semi-circle, cross-legged, and facing the audience.

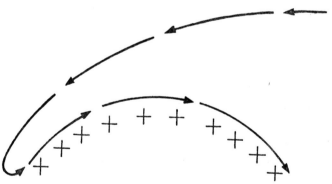

They all mime eating with alternate hands exactly on the musical beat, the greedy one (sitting up left centre) eats in double time; they mime drinking, putting glasses down, and they rise; the one who has over-eaten staggers across to down left holding his middle and falls, the others all point at him and hold the position in tableau.

VERSE 2

The Sailor Boys skip into position centre, five seated and four standing looking on in an uneven group. Those who are seated mime the dealing and playing of cards. They yawn and all of them go to sleep leaning on one another in various ways. At the sound of the alarm clock, all but one wake up and run and make a line across the front of the stage, leaving the one asleep down right. Exactly together they mime cleaning their teeth, then they put on their hats, turn to the left, and run off down left in single file.

VERSE 3

The Mermaid enters and sits down stage right miming combing her hair. The eight Sailor Boys skip from down left to up centre, forming themselves in a semicircle with the bulge towards the audience. With their backs to the audience, they mime digging sand and throwing sand over left shoulders, and one boy (just left-centre of the circle) catches sight of the Mermaid as he throws; slowly and shyly he walks across to her down right and sits at her feet; she chucks him under the chin. The others shade their eyes with their hands and stare shocked, holding tableau.

VERSE 4

The remaining Sailor Boys spread themselves into a jagged group, and mime chopping wood; one (fairly centrally placed) does double-sized chopping in half-time. The others stop chopping and watch, and when he 'chops himself in half' the impetus is so great that he spins in several circles to the left, as if the top half of his body were disconnected, and so he falls. The others stare at him in various characteristic attitudes and hold tableau.

VERSE 5

The Beehive comes in and stands up stage right. The Bee is already in position in the middle of the hive. The Sailor Boys dance round in a circle holding hands as if playing 'ring a ring o' roses'. One of them tries to join in the circle, but they won't let him, so he goes curiously to the Hive. The Bee buzzes out and chases him all round the circle of other boys (who are by now on the ground 'we all fall down'); the Bee stings the curious boy who falls right, and the Bee returns to the Hive. All the other Sailors' heads turn towards the one who has been stung, holding tableau.

VERSE 6

Four of the five remaining Sailor Boys move into position and then walk very slowly from up centre diagonally to left, standing solemnly in a line. They mime carrying enormous books, which they put down and open; they put on their spectacles, pick up the books and begin to read, standing in a line. One Sailor Boy walks down the line studying the covers and looking over the top of each book. When he gets to the fourth one, the reader closes the book, lifts it, knocks him on the head with it, and the boy falls—his legs flop to the ground on the last beat of the music; the others stare, holding tableau.

VERSE 7

The four Sailor Boys mime swimming in various ways and in various directions. One is doing a back crawl to the right From the right appears a large Fish; its jaws engulf the boy and they sweep him to up left. The others stare after him in tableau.

VERSE 8

At the opening of this music a Large Bear and a Baby Bear come in from up stage left and stand left centre; then two Penguins waddle in from up right, and stand right-centre. The three Sailor Boys come happily down-stage centre eating ice-cream, one of the boys offers some ice-cream to the Baby Bear, who comes down centre playing with him; the Mother Bear comes up behind, hugs the boy and carries him to left, both sitting on the floor.

VERSE 9

The two remaining Sailor Boys lie in imaginary sun, centre stage; one mimes being frizzled up by the sun, the other stares in horror.

VERSE 10

The Sailor Boy who is left, rises. The Story Teller stops the verse after the line: 'He got married'— then a little Bride enters from down right and joins the boy. As the music changes to the 'Wedding March', they walk slowly up stage centre with their backs to the audience. By this time the Parson has come from up stage left and is waiting for them centre back. They kneel, give the ring, rise:— Then the Story Teller speaks the lines:

> "He got married
> *and then there were——*"

At this all the nine Sailor Boys (excluding the tenth who stands centre with his bride) rise from their positions and run and sit in a row across the front of the stage, facing front: at the right end of the row we see there is a little girl in a sun-bonnet (who has come from down right). The Bride and Bridegroom (now suddenly the mother and father of a large family) count them from left to right, registering great surprise when they see that the tenth is a little girl! As each Sailor Boy is counted he turns his head to look at the little girl. The father looks disapproving, and the mother looks coy.

THE YOUNG KING

A mime based on a story by Oscar Wilde, with music composed by Barbara Lander.

This would be most suited to Seniors and Adults, but Juniors might well work freely on the story, without striving too hard with the technique required to interpret music and movement.

Characters

The Young King (a goat-herd)
His Companion (a boy lute-player)
The Archbishop
The Lord Chamberlain
The Usher
The Master of the Robes
The Master of Perfumes
Court Ladies (at least seven) ⎫
Court Gentlemen (at least six) ⎬ more if available
A Herald-trumpeter-boy ⎭
A Page (who is also the crown bearer)

In the Dream

The Chief Weaver
Two other Weavers
A Child Weaver
A Diver
An Octopus
Two miners
The Spirit of Fever

Set and Lighting

The scene should give an impression of spaciousness, so that the main part of it represents a Throne Room. Up stage left there are some steps leading to the throne itself. Down stage right and left are tables on which the Coronation robes are laid out for inspection. Slightly recessed up stage right are steps leading to an altar which is visible to the audience. Up stage centre there is an opening leading to other parts of the palace. A stool or two are placed easily down stage left right of centre. The room should have as lavish an appearance as possible.

The lighting must give us a natural interior, with beams of sun from windows right and left and from the entrance hall up stage centre. There will be candles on the altar and an extra light close to the throne which will be lit by the usher when he enters, put out as he exits, and lit again on his second entry.

After the entrance of the King and the trying on of the robes, the afternoon sun from the windows begins to diminish to evening, and the shadows lengthen, so that by the time the usher turns out the light by the throne it is nearly dark; there is still the reflection of a beam of moonlight from the window which makes the King and his companions visible.

The three dreams will appear in the three unoccupied corners of the stage; the weavers down stage left, the diver up stage right, and the miners down stage right, each of these corners will need to be separately lit, so that each scene can fade in and out from a black-out; similarly the throne must be lit separately, so that at the conclusion of each dream we are shown a glimpse of the restless King, even though the light is only brought half up.

At the end of the third dream the morning will be approaching, and the whole scene will grow gradually lighter as the sun comes up. By the time the Archbisop arrives, there will be full morning light.

At the moment of the crowning, there is thunder and a

sudden black-out. During the black-out a mantle will be flung round the King and his staff changed for another; this can be quickly and easily done, and as light is restored and the transformation of the King is shown— there must be a spot on the King; the rest of the stage need not be fully lit until the last moment before the curtain falls.

Costume

The Goat-herd-boy-King should be bronzed and good-looking and carry a staff, and he should wear skins. At the end of the play, when he is transformed, a full mantle should envelop him, and though it should have great simplicity and no jewels, it might be made to sparkle with an ethereal quality. His original staff will be changed, and the new one will have a lily blossom at the top.

The Court Characters can be of any period; I would suggest mediaeval.

The Dream Characters should be simply presented—*the weavers* as peasants of the period. *The octopus* all black with hanging pieces from legs and arms. *The diver* in tights, with a large transparent cover over his head and down to his waist, as in the old tapestries. *The miners* in tights and bare from the waist up. *The Spirit of Fever* can be shown in any free imaginative way, or simply in red body tights and a quivering head-dress.

Theme of the Play

There is much excitement at the Court today. The old King has died, and it is now known that a boy goat-herd living in a forest nearby is the rightful heir to the throne. The boy has been found, and is today being brought to the Court for the first time. "What will he be like? How will he behave?" These questions are on everybody's lips. This is the eve of the Coronation, and this evening the boy is coming to try on his ceremonial Coronation robes which are lavishly displayed about the Throne Room. As the curtain rises we have a glimpse of the room in quiet before any bustle and excitement begins. The rays of the afternoon sun heighten the colours of the beautiful robes spread out in readiness; the decorated throne, and small altar up the steps in a recess, both seem to have a feeling of preparedness for something great that is about to happen. Then, from another part of the palace, a boy herald arrives in the great centre opening to the room. He looks round for a moment, comes into the room, faces smartly up to the opening, lifts his trumpet to his lips and so summons the Court. He is followed closely by the Usher—a pompous and fussy gentleman—who, after lighting the lamp above the throne, surveys his preparations with some pride. He moves around to make sure that all is completely satisfactory, and, well pleased, he waits for the arrival of the rest of the Court. And now they come, beautiful ladies and gentlemen greet one another at the central opening, and swirl about the Throne Room adding still more to the air of anticipation; there is much gaiety among them, for whatever comes of it, this day is to be a great occasion!

Soon we see the Master of the Robes arriving; he is a busybody of a man, and seems to cause amusement to all as he bustles about absorbed in the finishing touches that must be put here and there, anxious that the crown and sceptre are in their proper place, and finally mingling with the crowd and making last plans with the Usher.

Now there is a little flutter among the ladies as the Master of Perfumes appears in the opening. Eagerly they push themselves forward into his path, and he sprays his perfume and talks to them charmingly as he passes. He is such a dandy that the gentlemen of the Court take little notice, but he attracts the ladies, and they enjoy his little 'asides' to them.

A very small page arrives and whispers to the boy herald that it is time to proclaim the arrival of the Lord Chamberlain; so the trumpet again blares forth, and the Lord Chamberlain with great dignity enters the Throne Room and acknowledges the greetings of all who are present. Now there is even more excitement, for the arrival of the Lord Chamberlain indicates that the King must be close behind. Final preparations are now made under the vigilant eye of the Lord Chamberlain, and when the general excitement is at its height, the herald trumpets the approach of the King.

The whole Court makes obeisance as the goat-herd King stands in the great centre opening. He feels lost for a moment, and turns to his young companion—the lute-player—who is close at his side. Never before has he seen such grandeur, and he is overwhelmed and over-awed by the loftiness of the room, the grand dresses, and the fact that everyone is bowing to him—a goat-herd. His young companion smiles encouragement and they pass down among the crowd to the Lord Chamberlain.

The Chamberlain now explains to the boy that he must try on his robes as a rehearsal for the great ceremony, and while he does so we have an opportunity to study the different reactions and characteristics of the Court ladies and gentlemen; some are sympathetic with the boy's youth, others are inclined to laugh at his ignorance, some think him uncouth, but many feel that he has a natural dignity and that there can be no doubt that he really is the King. Among the younger ladies there are some who are so interested in their own idle gossip and their little intrigues with the various Court gentlemen that they think of little else, and there are also older ladies and gentlemen who have learnt tolerance and give balance to the Court; all are present in the Throne Room for this occasion, and to everyone the occasion has significance.

The Master of the Robes takes charge of the dressing and fitting,—he is in a bustle of excitement, for him this is a moment of personal triumph, and the Master of Perfumes lends some assistance in his own particular languid way— while the Usher keeps an eye on the herald and the page who are almost ready to forget they are on duty, so exciting is it to them both that the new King should be so near to their own age. Some of the ladies and gentlemen offer assistance or comment, and the Lord Chamberlain stands by and directs when necessary. The boy King begins to enjoy his magnificent clothes, they are quite a novelty, and his companion is amused to see his mood changing; the page, bearing the crown on a velvet cushion comes and kneels at the feet of the King, but at this moment the Chamberlain directs that the gowns shall be removed and placed ready for the next day's ceremony. This done, he leads the young King to his throne and dismisses the Court.

Again the young King feels bewildered, he can hardly believe that he is sitting on this grand throne as all these beautiful ladies and elegant gentlemen curtsy and bow to him and pass out of the great hall; finally the Lord Chamberlain too bows his way out, and the boy is left with his companion. The King sinks back on his throne, hardly knowing what his feelings mean and his companion begins to play the lute. As a goat-herd boy he too had played out on the hillside alone with his flock; he now takes the lute himself and plays another dreamy tune. The evening grows darker, the feeling of peace and quiet spreads its influence and he falls asleep; gently the lute-player releases the instrument from him, puts down the lute and falls asleep himself on the steps of the throne.

The day has been exciting and the King sleeps restlessly;

he turns in his sleep and it is clear that his dreams are not making him happy. The room is quite dark now, and suddenly out of the dimness the sequence of his dreams is shown to us: Here is a horrifying dream. Some weavers are at work, obviously half-starved and driven; there is a child among them who keeps dropping asleep from hunger and exhaustion. They are weaving the material to make the robe for the King's Coronation. As they work, the chief weaver passes to and fro goading them on, he wakes the child, and a woman entreats him to be merciful. The chief weaver turns and strikes the woman, and she falls senseless; the child is worse off than before, the other weavers continue to work as if the incident was a normal one;—the dream fades —and we see the King again turning uncomfortably on his throne.

Then out of the shadows we see another dream tormenting him. A diver is in great danger at the bottom of the sea— feeling his way against the heavy weight of the water; he is experiencing difficulty, and cannot stay there much longer, but he must find a pearl for the King's crown. He opens an oyster and finds a pearl inside, and just as he is struggling to reach the surface an octopus appears out of the weeds behind him. For a moment he is off his guard, and the octopus has caught his leg in one of its long tentacles. The diver takes out his knife and battles for his life, but other tentacles close round him, all his struggles are in vain, he is engulfed and sinks on to the bed of the sea with the octopus.

The dream fades, and again we see the King discomforted and longing but unable to wake. His young companion is relaxed in sleep on the steps of the throne, blissfully unaware that he should have gone with the King to his bedchamber, for he too was exhausted and sleep came too easily.

Out of the shadows a third episode in this dream sequence

appears; this time there are two miners working in the humid heat of a river-bed; their job is to find rubies to deck the gown that the King is to wear at his Coronation. They are weary, and their searching brings no success.

Suddenly we are aware of a wraith or spirit that hovers quiveringly behind each man in turn; they stumble and breathe with difficulty and we realize that this is the spirit of fever—and as they continue to sweat and struggle, fever rises triumphant and both men die in the river-bed.

It is nearly morning when this dream fades, and the light of the dawn is already in the room. The King rouses himself from his nightmares; he starts up realizing he has been there all night; he sees the robes lying ready to wear, he darts across the room to look at them again. Yes, there is the exquisitely woven mantle, the pearls on the crown, the rubies decking the magnificent gown. How could he have worn them, even for a moment, with pleasure, the previous night! After his dreams he could not possibly do so again, it is too horrible. He will destroy them. The lute-player, now awakened by the King's violent movements, realizes that it is dawn and that he has slept there too long. He runs across, intending to help the King to dress. He is astonished to find him crumpling and tearing the precious garments. Anxiously the lute-player runs to the entrance and calls for help. The page and herald are soon on the scene; they were already nearly dressed, and run in pulling on their tunics as they come. Other members of the Court follow closely, for already they were expecting the arrival of the Archbishop for the ceremony.

The Master of Perfumes drifts leisurely in to see why the crowd is gathering; but when the Master of the Robes arrives he is distracted by the sight! All his exquisite workmanship to be treated like this! What hooligans! The Usher is equally worried and goes back to report to the Lord

Chamberlain, and there is general consternation. By the time the Chamberlain arrives the boy is beginning to explain his actions and tell his dreams. He is so moved by the thought that as he tells he half re-enacts all that he dreamt. At first the crowded court are mildly interested, some are amused, some are annoyed, but when the boy King ends his tale with a declaration that he will not wear any of the royal attire, then they are horrified. Some of the older people, thinking it is just a childish whim, try to pacify him kindly and tell him the effect of his dreams will soon pass; but he will not listen; the situation becomes more serious, and the Chamberlain exerts his authority and insists angrily that the usual procedure must be observed, and the boy must now dress quickly. To his astonishment the boy remains adamant, and says he will not be crowned at all unless it is in his own simple attire. At this juncture the herald trumpets the approach of the Archbishop, and the time for the Coronation has arrived. From the great central opening we see the Archbishop approach, followed by the crown-bearer, who takes the crown from the table, and carefully placing it on its cushion, stands in readiness for the Ceremony. The Court make a great obeisance as the Archbishop comes among them.

The Lord Chamberlain is in a dilemma; with a mixture of awkwardness and anger he tries to give the Archbishop a true idea of what has happened.

The Archbishop turns to the boy, it is clear that he appreciates his feelings, but he tries to persuade him kindly to follow the usual custom. Finding no response,—to the horror of many of the Court officials—and particularly the Master of the Robes—the Archbishop agrees that the crowning shall take place as the boy wishes and the fine robes are removed. Then the Archbishop leads the goat-herd boy to the foot of the altar steps, and the boy walks slowly up and kneels at the altar, followed by the Archbishop. As the boy rises, the Archbishop takes the crown and mounts the steps to the altar, and looking kindly at the boy he places the crown on his head. At this moment there is a clap of thunder, which causes panic among the crowd—what disaster can this be? What have they done to cause it? There is a sudden darkness and thunder; then gradually the altar is transfused with light that grows to a great brilliance and as the Archbishop moves away down the steps we see the boy King standing at the altar suddenly transformed, no longer a simple goat-herd, but dressed in a mantle more beautiful than any courtly robes, and in his hand, his goat-herd's staff is blossoming like a lily.

That this is a miracle everyone is sure, and in amazement and wonder all kneel in recognition, and in acknowledgement of their King. The Archbisop walks away from the altar to the back of the crowd, and he too kneels among them, showing that he recognizes the sign and the hand of God in the vision of this boy.

CHANGE OF HEART

A mime, only suitable I think, for Seniors or Adults.

The mime is in five episodes with an introduction and a finale, and is symbolic of War and its attendant evils.

Music for this play has been composed by Josephine Rhodes.[1]

Characters

A Man (symbolizing Man's Indifference)
A Woman (symbolizing The Spiritual Light of His Conscience)
Two small children
Three bigger boys
A poor girl
A poor man
A wealthy woman
A wealthy man
Another wealthy man
A nun
Two street orators
One Figure—symbolishing the War Machine. (This can be played equally well by one person or by several people)
Two blind people
Five refugees
Three cripples
Other war victims
Children. Passers-by
Makers of armaments
Other members of the crowd

---

[1] The music is the composer's copyright, but may be obtained on hire. Anyone wishing to do so should apply to Miss Josephine Rhodes, 40 Nevilles Court, Dollis Hill Lane, N.W.2, or to The Rose Bruford College, Lamorbey Park, Sidcup, Kent.

Set and Lighting

As one episode must run without pause or curtain into the next, there can be very little help from the set; all that is necessary is a curtain set with cyclorama or sky-cloth behind, so that it is possible to have either an open stage, or closed curtains at the back, which may partially open for a particular episode or effect. An easily portable bench and a street lamp can be placed in the black-out for some of the episodes. In front of the proscenium arch and as far away from the main acting area as possible is a small table and chair. This remains throughout the play. Hand properties such as cards, bottles, marbles, can be real, but armaments, etc., should be mimed.

The lighting is of great importance. There are certain special areas of light:

(*a*) The large acting area, with a pool of light round the lamp-post when it is used.

(*b*) The area between drapes and cyclorama when there is an effect like the War Machine up stage centre, also for the finale.

(*c*) The table and chair outside the proscenium.

There will be a black-out between each episode and the slight change of set can then be made. Simultaneously with the black-out on the acting area the light on the table and chair will be brought up so that we see Man and his conscience between every episode; this fades again as each episode is played, except in the Introduction, in Episode V and in the Finale.

LIGHTING AND SETTINGS FOR SEPARATE EPISODES

Introduction: Man and his Conscience lit, the rest of stage in darkness.

Episode 1. Open stage and cyclorama—normal light of day.

Episode 2. Open stage and cyclorama—street lamp placed right centre of stage towards back—bench placed up stage towards left centre.

Episode 3. Open stage and cyclorama. Bench placed left centre of stage. Orators bring on their own tub and place it right centre of stage. Lighting as for an open-air scene on a sunny day.

Episode 4. The curtains are closed across the back, and the lighting as for an interior in the afternoon, without regard for sources of light, windows, etc., as the scene is abstract.

At a given cue the curtains at the back part, disclosing the War Machine high on a rostrum, and in silhouette, with a red glow on the cyclorama and some red on the stage, too. Towards the end of the scene almost all in silhouette.

Episode 5. The curtains are closed across the back. There is not much light at the beginning of the scene but enough to differentiate clearly between the characters. In this scene the light on Man at the table is full up throughout.

Finale and Resolution. At a given cue the curtains at the back part, disclosing the light of Man's Conscience dominating the scene from the rostrum in the opening (used earlier by the War Machine); there is a strong light on this figure and gradually the light increases on the whole scene until the final curtain.

Theme of the Play

INTRODUCTION

A man sits at a table at the side of the stage, if possible outside the proscenium; he is separated from the scenes that follow. The man is good-looking and as we see him now we feel he could inspire confidence, and be a leader of men. He is playing cards, but as he plays it becomes evident that he is bored with his life; the game is not going

as he wishes, so he stops playing and throws a dice; he
takes a drink from the bottle on his table, lights a drugged
cigarette, continues his card game, and we realize that
he typifies Indifference. Standing close behind his chair
is a beautiful woman; she observes him closely, but whereas
at first he seemed aware of her presence as he drinks he loses
that awareness and she can no longer influence him; she
turns away; she is the Spiritual Life of his Conscience. The
light fades from them and comes up on:

EPISODE I.   INDIVIDUALISM

Two children are happily playing marbles; they are not
very old and are obviously happy about the new marbles
they have acquired and are enjoying their game. While they
play, three bigger boys come along and see what is happening; they have no marbles of their own, so decide they will
bully the little ones, and make them give them up. They
set on the children from behind, take their marbles and
tease them, finally running away and leaving the players
disconsolate, one angry and the other very near to tears.
As the light fades on this scene, we are again aware of Man
and his Conscience for a few moments. Man is obviously
affected by what he has seen; he is sorry to see the bullies
win, but the episode is over, he shrugs his shoulders, takes
another drink and continues to play.

EPISODE 2.   CLASS RIVALRY AND HATRED

We now see a poor girl standing under a lamp at a street
corner, obviously anxiously waiting for someone. In a few
moments she is joined by a young man; she meets and greets
him eagerly, but he shows her he has had no luck, the work
he wanted and tried for he did not get and he has no money
left. He catches sight of a cigarette end lying in the gutter
and eagerly picks it up and smokes it. At this moment a

man and woman in evening dress pick their way across the street obviously looking for a taxi. The unemployed young man stands quietly and his girl goes towards the woman pleading for money; the wealthy man is annoyed that his lady should be troubled in this way and brushes the girl aside. She is so weak that she falls to the ground as the couple pass off. Her young man is incensed and goes to help her up; they sit on the bench. From lower down the street another wealthy and unpleasant-looking man appears, the girl again goes forward to plead for help, but hesitates when she sees the man alone. He stops, puts his monocle to his eye and looks her up and down; he comes closer to her, offering her money if she will go with him. She is horrified and instinctively steps back and appeals to her young man friend; then, realizing how great their need is she moves as if to accept the money and the conditions. At this, the young man can bear it no more and knocks the man down. He falls and they realize he is dead.

As this scene fades, we are again aware of the effect on Man and his Conscience. For a moment his card game is arrested and we hope he is moved, but again he shelves his responsibility, drinks to the future, and plays again, as the lights fade and we see:

EPISODE 3.   PROPAGANDA

The scene has changed, and we are in a park; on the bench left is a nun surrounded by a group of children; they are absorbed in a story she is reading to them. The peace of this scene is rudely interrupted by the entry of two street orators carrying a tub; one of them mounts this and begins to address passers-by, while the other helps to collect the crowd. Gradually more and more people collect, and the children become more interested in the speaker than in the nun's story. The theme of the speech is 'Build up wealth for yourselves by making armaments'. One by one the children are prevailed upon to join the crowd right, and as the speech reaches its climax and the scene fades we realize that only one child was left listening to the nun.

Again we see Man struggling with his Conscience, but he plays and drinks with abandon and becomes the epitome of Indifference as we continue into:

EPISODE 4. WAR

The scene opens on a large group of people whose movements make us aware that this is an armament factory; all are now busily employed. When the activity is at its height —the light changes and brings to life the next part of this scene. The curtains have parted at the back, and a magnificent and dreadful figure high above the workers dominates everything. This is the War Machine driving everyone to final destruction. A red glow suffuses the scene and before it completely fades there is a silhouette showing that the workers have become a mass of humanity struggling and fighting furiously; the movement gathers speed and impetus and ends with general destruction and despair.

The light dies and Man is seen again, but this time he is alone, his Conscience has left him. He is half drunk, he has stopped playing and is in a state of terror; he madly throws his dice, but nothing can help him now and he remains visible and part of the scene as we move into:

EPISODE 5. AFTERMATH

Gradually, one or two at a time, we see a procession of suffering humanity filling the stage. Here come the cripples, the wounded, the blind, the refugees; it seems that all the world's sorrow is here. As the group grows it is noticeable that all their eyes are turned in one direction, they are staring or pointing at the Indifferent Man who has played and drunk

o

his life away, ignoring all that led to this moment. As he feels all their eyes upon him, he can bear it no more. He leaves his table and rushes to the centre of the crowd, but feeling himself surrounded, he struggles to free himself and rushes to each corner in turn only to meet reproachful eyes which he cannot pass, until at last he falls in a heap in despair and remorse.

At last his better feelings have been aroused, at a great cost, and now:

FINALE AND RESOLUTION

The curtains up stage centre part and in place of the War Machine we see the Spiritual Life of Man's Conscience high above the scene, radiantly pointing out to the light and the way to Peace. The Man slowly raises his head, feeling that there is a difference; he slowly turns, recognizes his Conscience, and the truth is clear to him at last. He moves up to her, and as the curtain falls we see that he is moving up towards the light.

VILLAGE CONCERT

A comedy mime for Seniors and Adults, with music composed by Barbara Lander.

Characters

Farmer Briggs
His Son
The Lady of the Manor
Joe (the boxer)
Little Willie
Miss Hoodwink (the pianist)
Mr Hardy (the schoolteacher)
The Squire
The Vicar
His Wife
Little Millicent
Her Mother
Her Father
Jack (the sailor)
Maisie ⎫
Primrose ⎭ His girl-friends

Other members of the orchestra (as many as desired)
Members of the Audience (at least sixteen and more if possible)

Set and Lighting

The set should consist of a raised platform diagonally across the corner up stage left, for orchestra and performers, with an entrance from one side or at the back of this platform. A few chairs should be placed ready for the orchestra at the beginning. Chairs for the audience should be placed in rows facing the platform, half backing the audience, from down stage right to centre, on diagonal lines.

An entrance for the audience from up stage right.

The lighting is uncomplicated, a fairly sunny interior, with a shaft of light as if from a window giving the platform a little more illumination than the rest.

Costume

Modern dress, a little old-fashioned perhaps, and noticeably suggesting the characters as described.

Theme of the Play

At the opening we see an ordinary bare village-hall, with a low platform at one end; the scene is quickly brought to life by the characters who use it:

The first to arrive is Farmer Briggs, so deaf that he didn't hear what time the concert was to begin. But he always makes a point of being early and he is eager to start, for he plays leading fiddle in the village orchestra. While he is getting out his instrument and settling down, his son, George, arrives—a robust, solemn young man, who follows in his father's footsteps, for he plays second fiddle.

Now comes the Lady of the Manor. She is very popular with everyone, but they are all conscious of the honour she bestows in deigning to join the orchestra. She is a horse-woman who seems to ride the 'cello much as she would ride to hounds. When she plays, she thrashes it with vigour, keeping the pace if not always the time.

Presently they are joined by Joe, the boxer, who 'doubles' the triangle and the mouth-organ—and a very sensitive player he is too. With him comes Little Willie, the publican's son: though somewhat awed by the galaxy of local 'stars', he is none the less proud of his accomplishments as drummer, and he is the envy of all the other village-boys.

While they and other members of the orchestra are preparing for the 'fray', and only just in time, arrives Miss Hoodwink, pianist of local renown. For many years the

'May Queen', she has now passed her prime, but retains every bit of her self-confidence. Importantly she strikes the 'A' and the orchestra are busy tuning up as the audience arrives full of expectancy and excitement. All the village is there, and there is a bustle of anticipation as they murmur good wishes to the relatives and friends of performers, admire the programme girls and fight for the best seats.

Then the Squire enters, accompanied by the Vicar and the Vicar's wife. They sail into their reserved seats in the front row, and all is ready to begin.

Finally, Mr Hardy, the schoolteacher, walks impressively on to the platform and takes his place as conductor. Miss Hoodwink glares at him forbiddingly for she has a fixed idea that it is her job to keep the orchestra together and she has little respect for conductors. There is always battle between these two and the allegiance of the members of the orchestra is divided, though they work with a will following the one or the other. The orchestra opens with an impassioned rendering of a familiar 'number' in which their energy and effort are displayed to advantage. They receive an ovation from the thrilled audience and, flushed with success, they move back to make room on the platform for other performers.

On comes tiny red-haired Millicent, beautifully beribboned for the occasion, to recite her poem. Alas, she forgets and hesitates, but after making a fresh start, she attains sufficient impetus to carry her through to a triumphant end and the audience happily applaud the young prodigy. Her mother and father now take the stage (accepting applause with modest awareness that they are really a brilliant family). They sing their duet, given 'by request' in accordance with tradition.

Now we reach the high-spot of the evening—Jack, the sailor, hero of the village, is home on leave. Mounting the platform, he delights the girls with a brilliant execution of the 'hornpipe'. The applause is vociferous and he obliges with an encore and finally dances his way off the platform to further deafening applause.

The Vicar now rises and raises his hand for silence. Beaming benevolently, he makes an earnest appeal for the advertised charity, cracking his customary joke in conclusion. A collection is taken, and Mr Hardy returns to his position to conduct the orchestra in their final selection. After more applause, the audience begins to disperse. But who are these young ladies lingering behind, some supported by hopeful parents? They are waiting for Jack, vying with each other for the honour of his escort, much to the chagrin of the other lads of the village, who stand self-consciously by, doing their best to register indifference. Suddenly he appears from the back, but—what dismay!—he is not alone. With him are Maisie and Primrose who are strangers to the village. He bounces cheerfully out of the hall with a girl on each arm, the astonished group staring after him. Disconsolately they wander out, and the last member of the orchestra leaves the hall.

Note. The fun of this mime is in the clear characterization and the miming of the instruments—no props *at all* should be used—only chairs.

THE PLAGUE

An abstract mime suitable for performance by Seniors and Adults.

This would be effective if accompanied by sounds—e.g. drum, pipe and some human sounds such as singing or humming, laughter, hissing, or murmurs, also sudden moments of complete silence.

Characters

The Burgomaster
A Pedlar
A Friar
A Quack doctor
A Nun
A Boy who plays a pipe
Three abstract figures (representing Plague)
A crowd of mediaeval ladies and gentlemen
Some children

Set and Lighting

The scene is a mediaeval market-place with an entrance between the houses up stage right; there are also entrances from right and left. If possible some of the upper windows of the houses should be practical, so that at some moments villagers can watch the happenings in the market-place from above. There is an old well down left.

The lighting should convey the mood rather than the reality of the play, starting off with the bright sunlight of the morning, growing strange and dark for the entrance of Plague, but still light enough for us to see all the characters clearly; at the end the sunlight will return.

Costume

Plague may be represented as shrouded black figures, or in

black body-tights and masks, according to the conception of the producer.

The other characters in mediaeval costume.

Theme of the Play

It is early morning in this mediaeval market-place; house-doors are opening and people pass by happily greeting one another as they pass. A woman is singing as she cleans her courtyard; a boy, also singing, goes to the well to fetch water and returns to his house. Some children are playing in a little group on the right. Presently there is the sound of a small drum-beat, and a young pedlar comes into view, beating a drum to attract attention to himself and the wares he has to sell. The children stop their game and crowd round him laughing gaily. The pedlar is generous and gives them some trinkets to play with. One of the boys has been given a pipe which he begins to play and some of the children find themselves dancing and gradually men and women come from their houses to watch and join in.

Buying and selling is at its height when the Burgomaster passes by. He is much respected by all the citizens and they give him a great welcome.

The scene is at its gayest when an old friar joins the crowd; as he comes among them the mood changes, for he brings news that in a neighbouring village there is plague and many people are dying. The children do not understand why their mothers and fathers suddenly look so serious and quiet, but the dancing comes to a standstill and the tune on the pipe has changed to a minor key; the day is clouding over and a shiver passes through the crowd. It seems as if there is a faint hissing sound in the air although the crowd seem to hear nothing. Now we see three weird figures creeping among the people like shadows. No one can see them, but we see that they hover as a hawk hovers before seizing its prey. One by one they find their victim and stand close by like a shadow and immediately the victims are stricken with plague and fall to the ground, contaminated; no one dares touch them, and terror runs through the crowd. The boy with the pipe is taken with plague and his father runs for the quack doctor, who quickly comes and performs various rites; but in the middle of the cure, one of the shadows crosses his path; the quack doctor too has the plague and terror grows to panic. Many of the crowd creep back to their homes. A few of the people stay with a nun who has remained quiet and tranquil throughout; her faith revives their fearful spirits. Plague is defeated, the three figures lose their power and pass on to the next village.

Slowly life returns to its normal round. It is as though a cloud has passed by; and the singing is resumed as before, but it is a different voice, for she who sang before was a victim of the plague; but life continues.

*   *   *

Now follow four mimes which have been worked out by my students, by whose kind permission I am using them in this book.

THE FRENCH HAT SHOP

This depends very largely on precision of music and movement, and the student who worked it out has quoted music
she thought suitable, but naturally permission would have to
be granted by the music publishers before using it, so the
ideas should only be used as an indication of the kind of
music required.

This little play could be effective in smart French costume, but it can be even more amusing if performed in
a simple basic costume. The only furniture needed is
two chairs and a table. Doors, hats, handbags, etc., are
mimed.

This could be performed by Juniors, Seniors or Adults,
but again Juniors would approach it more realistically and
without the same stylized precision as older and more
sophisticated actors.

Characters

Madame
Her two assistants
A plump, frivolous lady
A slender, sophisticated lady

The scene is set in an exclusive millinery shop in Paris.
It is essentially modern; with swing doors of plate glass down
stage centre, and thick carpets on the floor. Two gilt chairs
face the audience, one on either side of the entrance. Between
them is a small, elegant table.

1. As the curtain rises Madame is standing down centre
(facing the imaginary swing doors) filing her beautifully
kept nails. Up left and up right her two assistants are un-
packing hats. As they do so they cannot resist trying on one

or two of the latest creations, but unfortunately Madame turns round and sees them. Scandalized she hurries over, tears the hats off their heads and shakes her arms in despair.

2. Just then a customer is seen. Immediately Madame adopts her poise and charm again. The plump, frivolous lady enters, walking in very high heels with short, tapping steps. She wears a tight skirt, carries a dainty, if useless, handbag and wears an enormous hat. Pushing open the swing doors she is ushered into the shop by Madame and shown to the chair left centre. Taking off her large hat and placing it on the centre table she sits down, gracefully crossing her ankles.

Madame says, "What can I show you?"

The plump, frivolous lady replies, "I want a small hat with a frilly veil."

Madame turns to No. 1 of her assistants and repeats, "She wants a small hat with a frilly veil."

As if to impress it firmly in her mind the assistant says, "Yes, a small hat with a frilly veil"—and she finds one. She brings it to the customer and places it on her head.

But the plump, frivolous lady isn't sure that she likes it (Madame and the staff secretly think it hideous), but when she turns for confirmation of her doubts—"Voilà —it is exquisite!" She tries hard to believe this statement but regretfully says, "Non. What else can I be shown?"

3. But now enters another customer—a slender, sophisticated lady. She is superbly dressed. She walks slowly and languishingly. Madame shows her to the chair right centre. Taking off her small, dainty hat she places it on the centre table and sits down.

Madame says, "What can I show you?"

The slender, sophisticated lady replies, "I want a large hat with flowers on it."

As if to impress it firmly on her mind assistant No. 2. says, "Yes, a large hat with flowers on"—and she finds one. She brings it to the customer and places it on her head.

But, no, it is not satisfactory.

4. Then both ladies turn together and see each other's hats on the centre table.

Ah! At last!

Simultaneously they pick them up and try them on. Exquisite! They beckon the assistants (Madame stays up centre, horrified), pick up their handbags, open their cheque books and write and sign. They stand and prepare to leave, but as they are well satisfied customers in a friendly mood they go out arm in arm through the swing doors. Madame stands centre holding their cheques.

5. Outside the two ladies pause to admire each other's hats—then they recognize them as their own! Angry, the plump, frivolous lady snatches her hat away; the slender, sophisticated lady does the same, and then they realize they have been cheated. With one accord they march back into the shop where Madame is still standing holding the cheques. Together they snatch them away, place the hats back into her hands, tear up the cheques, and confident that wrong has been righted they stalk out of the milliner's—(hatless!)—and go their separate ways.

6. Madame, flabbergasted, throws the hats into the air with a final, "Ah, well!"

Notes on Music

Music suggested:

Piano selection from *Bless the Bride* by Vivian Ellis, published by Chappell, and *Carousel* by Richard Rodgers, published by Williamson Music Ltd.

1. *Carousel:* 'What's the use of Wond'rin' (Madame and her
      two assistants)

Introduction   9th and 10th Bars

Begin at 1st bar

Madame files her nails. Assistants unpack hats   4 Bars

They try them on   6 Bars

Repeat last 10 bars angrily

Madame sees them   2 Bars

Runs to them   2 Bars

Snatches hat off assistant No. 1   1 Bar

Snatches hat off assistant No. 2   1 Bar

Looks at both reprovingly. Shakes arms in despair   4 Bars

2. *Bless the Bride:* 'Ma Belle Marguerite' (Plump, frivolous lady)

Cut first 6 bars and begin on 7th

Plump, frivolous lady enters   2 Bars

Opens swing doors   2 Bars

Ushered to seat by Madame   2 Bars

Takes off hat   1 Bar

And sits   1 Bar

Madame says, "What can I show you?"   2 Bars

Plump, frivolous lady says, "I want a small hat
      with a frilly veil."   Play trill in place of next 2 Bars

Madame to assistants, "She wants a small hat with
      a frilly veil."   Repeat trill octave higher

Assistant 1. "Yes, a small hat with a frilly veil."
                                       Same, octave higher

Assistant 1. Brings hat and places it on plump,
      frivolous lady's head   4 Bars

Plump, frivolous lady looks doubtful. So do
      Madame and the assistants   1 Bar

Plump, frivolous lady turns to them, but, "Ah, it
      is exquisite!"   1 Bar

Plump, frivolous lady returns to mirror and
      shakes head   2 Bars

Cut last 4 bars of piece

3. *Bless the Bride:* 'Table for Two'. (Slender, sophisticated lady)

Slender, sophisticated lady enters	3 Bars
Open swing doors	1 Bar
Shown to chair by Madame	3 Bars
Takes off hat	1 Bar
Madame says, "What can I show you?"	3 Bars
Slender, sophisticated lady says, "I want a large hat with flowers."	Insert trill
Madame says, "She wants a large hat with flowers."	Trill octave higher
Assistant 2. "Yes, a large hat with flowers on."	Trill octave higher still

Assistant 2. Brings hat and the slender, sophisticated lady tries it on ⎫
She studies it carefully, but regretfully, "Non" ⎬ Cut 4 bars and play the following 8

4. *Bless the Bride:* 'Oh, what will mother say?'

Plump, frivolous lady and slender, sophisticated lady see each other's hats on centre table

Cut first 4 bars and begin on 5th

Together: "Oh! How wonderful!"	2 Bars
Try the hats on	2 Bars
"Yes, it suits me."	2 Bars
"Exquisite!" Beckon assistants	2 Bars
Open bags, take out cheque books	4 Bars
Receive pens	2 Bars
Sign	4 Bars
Tear out cheques and fasten bags	2 Bars

Repeat last 12 bars

See each other's hats	1 Bar
"It is mine"	1 Bar
Plump, frivolous lady walks left and takes her hat	2 Bars

Slender, sophisticated lady walks right and takes
    hers   2 Bars
Point at shop, push swing doors open and enter 6 Bars
Repeat last 8 *bars*
Together take cheques from Madame and return
    hats   2 Bars
Tear cheques   2 Bars
Open swing doors
Throw pieces away and exit, each a separate way 2 Bars

5. *Carousel:* 'What's the use of Wond'rin'. Play 1st, 2nd
and 8th bars and the first chord of the 9th bar. Madame
throws hats up. "Ah, well!"

THE CIRCUS

This play could be attempted by Juniors or Seniors. Some
adult classes might enjoy doing it if accustomed to a good
deal of movement.

Characters

The Ringmaster	3 Clowns
6 Horses	Girl equestrienne
Tamer of seals	Weight-lifter
3 Seals	Tight-rope walker
Fish-man	Children (audience)

Music

I would again suggest well-known songs, a change of
theme for each new character or group of characters.

Setting, Lighting, and Costume

While it is obvious that elaborate setting, lighting, and
costumes could be used, the scene could I think be more
effective with an empty stage and basic practice costume,

allowing the miming only to rouse the imagination of the audience. Suggestions of costume might help the effect as in 'The Ten Little Sailor Boys', e.g. a cloak for the ring-master, funny hats for the clowns, sunshade for the tight-rope walker.

The scene opens with a group of excited children sitting on the floor in a circle, with a space up stage centre. Their excitement increases as the characters of the circus enter.

First comes the Ringmaster. He wears a cloak and comes with a great flourish, bowing to everyone on all sides and introducing his troupe. Then he calls on his beautiful prancing horses, six of them, high steppers with beautiful heads tossing as they come; he commands them and round and round the ring they go, then off again.

Next come the performing seals, three of them, wriggling their way into the centre, using their flippers to propel themselves along, following the directions of their tamer. He throws a big ball to them and they bounce it on their noses from one to the other. At the end of their performance he sends for some fish, which is brought in by the fish-man, and he throws them their reward before they go out, accompanied by great applause, and applauding themselves by flapping their fins.

Then come three clowns, riding on each other's shoulders, laughing at their knockabout jokes, climbing through hoops, making the children laugh to the end.

Then the girl equestrienne is seen coming; she is standing on her horse, riding bare-back, just like a dancer, as exciting as any trapeze artist.

When she has gone there is the weight-lifter with his immense muscles making all marvel at his strength.

Then comes the little lady with her sunshade who walks on a tight-rope, miraculous and breath-taking; but she ends safely and bows her way out.

Back come the prancing horses and all the performers, taking their final bow as they circle and go off, the high-stepping horses making a final circle.

MACHINES

A mime suitable for juniors, seniors or adults.

Again basic practice costume could be used, and a bare stage, which would be helped by a silhouette effect in the lighting.

No music—the appropriate sounds to be made by the actors themselves.

Action

We now see characters grouped in twos, threes or fours, each representing a machine. Some are wheels, others pneumatic drills, or pumps or automatic slot machines. As they begin to move, each group separately, they make their own sound, so that no music is needed. The sounds are appropriate and varied, and the rhythms of the machines are fitted round a basic slow steady beat,—though they may be in time, or double, triple or even syncopated time.

The machine making the smallest noise starts first, and is gradually joined by the others according to size and noise. When all the groups are in action the rhythm is intensified and quickened, and suddenly, at the height of the excitement, a whistle is blown, and the machines die away in softer noise and slower movement, and remain static as they were at the beginning.

THE PLAGUES OF EGYPT

An abstract mime which could be attempted by Juniors, Seniors or Adults, provided they know the Bible story of the Plagues of Egypt. Again a bare stage and basic practice costume is all that is needed. No music—appropriate sounds to be made by the actors themselves and the effect of thunder and lightning off stage.

Characters

> Egyptian Father
> Egyptian Mother
> Egyptian First-born Son
> Frogs, Flies and Lice and Locusts
> The River Nile
> Thunder and Lightning

Some of the characters represent the River Nile, lying on their backs and gently undulating their arms.

An Egyptian family enter, man, wife, and son, and walk slowly to the river to fill their water-jars, but as they stoop to do so they draw back in horror, finding their jars are being filled with blood. They throw them away in disgust. Then the frogs appear; four or five of them croaking and leaping around. The Egyptians mime that they are treading on others and surrounded by them, and the frogs group themselves on one side. Next comes the plague of flies and lice, buzzing and hissing and jumping with darting movements—the Egyptian family desperately trying to avoid them, until the insects settle in another group. The next plague is of boils, a horrible sequence in which the Egyptians feel great pain as the boils appear on their arms, necks and bodies. After this some terrifying figures enter, darting and flashing in every direction—these are thunder and lightning. Then the locusts appear, hovering with outstretched wings, finally settling in another group. The next group is slow and mysterious in movement—and a darkness comes ominously from the back of the stage. It seems that the Egyptians cannot suffer any more, but the most terrible punishment is still to come in the smiting down of the first-born. Slowly the son collapses and lies dead, leaving the parents grief-stricken in each other's arms.

Now follow two examples of solo mimes.

SOLO MIMES

SEVEN YEARS BAD LUCK
or
UPS AND DOWNS IN THE KITCHEN

Costume—A maidservant of the 1930s.
Set—A kitchen. Natural interior light.

As almost all the properties are mimed, a curtain set is quite adequate, as long as there is a chair and a small table with a cloth on it to the left of centre and a magazine lying on the table; also a standing-mirror somewhere handy which can be brought to the table, and an effect off stage for a knock at the door and also for breaking glass at the moment when the mirror falls.

Tray, crockery, cigarette, matches, comb, meat, cat, etc., should be mimed, and of course the butcher-boy is shown only by the girl's reaction. Choose a gay tune for the main action; change to three sentimental up-to-date songs for the three film stars, and on the entrance of the butcher-boy something as obviously appropriate as 'Oh, Johnny, Oh, Johnny, how you can love . . .'—then back to your original gay tune after his exit and for the end.

Action

The scene opens on an empty kitchen. Then from up stage left we see Lily, the maidservant, kick the door open and come in, carrying a tray of crockery. As she crosses the room with her head held high, she trips over the cat, and down she goes, crockery and all. That cat has always been a trouble, and this time he is literally her downfall! Lily shakes her fist at him as he slinks away, and then she ruefully looks at the pieces. She collects the upturned china and gathers it

together again on the tray, painfully aware of her bruises
as she does so; then she picks up the broken tea-pot. She
tries the pieces together, but it is too splintered and would
never stick. And now, oh dear! She hears footsteps and
recognizes her mistress's step. Quickly she jumps up, puts
the tray on a side-table, hides the broken pieces in a drawer
and stands waiting; but it was a false alarm, no one comes.
With a shrug of relief Lily takes off her cap, sits down at the
table near the fire, picks up the magazine that lies there and
begins to read. What bliss! Dare she smoke? That would
make this moment perfect; she would feel dreadfully aban-
doned! She would enjoy that too! She delves in the pocket
of her apron and out comes half a cigarette which she has
picked up, and a box of matches. She lights the cigarette and
smokes, sighs with delight, crosses her legs, picks up the
magazine and acts the grand ladies she has seen upstairs; but
after a few minutes she finds the cigarette is not quite as
good as she expected, so she takes it out, throws it in the
fire, and contents herself with her magazine, which we see
clearly from the cover is concerned with films.

As Lily turns the pages we see by her absorbed interest,
her obvious admiration and her envious sighs, that she has
aspirations and would like at least to look like a film star.
Suddenly she runs for the mirror, stands it on the table in
front of her and stares first at herself and then at a picture in
the book. From her apron pocket she produces a comb and
arranges her hair, her eye-brows and her mouth, to look like
a serious beauty, finally standing and adopting a slinky
mannequin-like line of body to match. But, alas! she catches
sight of her effort in the mirror and sinks down dejectedly.
It's no use, she can never be that type.

She turns to another page; here is obviously a gay young
thing, full of life and a tap-dancer, perhaps this would be
more suitable. Rapidly another hair-style is tried, the mouth

and eye-brows go up instead of down. She gets up, leaves the table and with the picture for a model in one hand she starts to dance, imagining her audience before her and world success. But this too comes to a sad end, for at her great moment she trips over her own feet and disconsolately sits again, deciding that dancing is not perhaps, after all, her strongest point.

Another page is turned and it is clear that this time she has seen a 'fluffy' blonde with a beautiful smile, one silk-stockinged leg crossed over the other, reclining in a deck-chair with pussy on her shoulder. "This is my chance", thinks Lily, and once again hair and face are arranged, and her dear friend the cat can at last come into his own. He is persuaded to play his part, and Lily is just developing the right feeling, when there is a rat-tat at the door. Now who is going to disturb her fun? The cat leaps away, Lily takes another look in the mirror and very conscious of the charm she is exuding crosses grandly to the door down stage right and opens it with a flourish. How opportune! Here is the butcher-boy, what could be better! Lily takes the meat, smells it suspiciously, crosses to the table, transfers the meat on to a plate, smiling encouragingly to the boy as she does so. Then she languidly returns to the door with the basket, which she hands back with 'invitation' in her eyes. Leaving the door open, she crosses to the front of the table and sits on the edge, beckoning the butcher-boy to come and join her. He needs no encouragement, and soon they are both perched on the edge and it is clear that they are enjoying a little affair. At the moment when enjoyment is at its height, Lily suddenly feels something behind her on the table; she turns and leaps away quickly. Horror! The cat is eating the meat! Lily claps her hands to distract him, but he is too deeply engaged, so she picks him up and throws him to the ground. Once more she hears her mistress's footsteps and she hurries to push the butcher-boy out of the door, reluctantly waving him away as he goes down the street. Then she runs for the meat, throws out offending pieces, hurriedly looks for somewhere to hide it, and without hesitation runs to the oven down stage left, pops the meat inside and slams the door. Still running, she gets to the table, picks up her cap and puts it on her head, hides the magazine under the tablecloth, BUT, in doing so, sends the mirror flying to the ground and sees it lying there smashed to atoms. As the curtain falls, Lily sinks into her chair, showing that she realizes that this time it means 'Seven Years' Bad Luck'.

THE JUGGLER

A mime based on the story of 'Our Lady of Notre Dame', suitable for seniors and adults.

Music for this mime has been arranged by Josephine Rhodes.[1]

The Set may be simple or elaborate and should represent the precincts of the Cathedral of Notre Dame, close to the porch, above which is a statue of the Virgin; the statue is off stage down right.

The Lighting should convey late afternoon and the setting sun should illuminate the juggler's face at the end of the play.

The Costume is that of a mediaeval juggler.

Properties should all be mimed, and the monks shown only by the reaction of the juggler.

(If so desired, this could become a group mime by introducing a group of monks, and the statue of the Virgin which will come to life.)

[1] Anyone wishing to hire copies of this music should apply to Miss Josephine Rhodes, 40 Nevilles Court, Dollis Hill Lane, N.W.2, or to The Rose Bruford College, Lamorbey Park, Sidcup, Kent.

Theme of the Play

As the scene opens an old juggler enters from up stage left; he carries a bundle which contains his equipment for his juggling, and he looks so weary that we wonder if he can travel any further. He looks round at the Cathedral Close and settles down with some relief to rest, centre stage. It is obvious that he is getting old and tired of life, and this quiet spot seems to him to be a sanctuary. Just as he is settling down to sleep, he hears voices approaching from off left; he realizes it is the monks coming to the Cathedral for their evening prayers. Quickly he gathers himself together, opens his bag, gets out his balls and prepares himself to juggle for them, so that he can earn a few coins to save him from starvation.

Now the monks come into view and stop to watch the juggler's antics, but suddenly he is overcome with fatigue and hunger and falls to the ground, fainting. Two of the monks run to his assistance, one produces a flask of water, another a crust of bread, and gradually the juggler is restored and able to rise to his feet and thank his kind friends. At this moment the Cathedral bell rings out inviting them to service, and one by one the monks make their way into the Cathedral, down stage right. The last to leave turns and asks the juggler to join them; he hesitates, but refuses; to him it would not be natural, he would feel out of place and awkward; to go to church is not his custom.

The monks have gone, the juggler is left alone; he seems to be feeling a little sad and wishes he had taken the chance to go with the monks. He peers into the Cathedral but does not dare to enter; he looks up at the statue of the Virgin above the porch, crosses himself and wonders what he can do for her; he seems to have so little to offer. Suddenly he thinks of his juggling; of course, that is all he has to offer, and that he will give her. Excitedly he gathers up his balls

and his pole to balance on his nose, all his best tricks shall
be shown to her. This shall be the finest performance he has
ever given! He sets to work, he juggles, balances, dances,
does every trick he knows, using all his energy in his effort
to worship the Virgin in the best way he can; but now the
monks come from the Cathedral and they are astonished to
find the juggler, looking up at the Virgin, and, as they
think, dancing irreverently in the Cathedral Close. Is this his
gratitude? Did they tend and succour him only to have their
religion flouted in this way? Angrily two of them take off
their girdles and begin to scourge him; he must be punished.

Weary with his efforts and not able to comprehend what
wrong he has done, the juggler once more sinks down
exhausted, and it seems that he will be whipped to death.
But the Virgin has accepted his prayer and by the reaction of
the monks he realizes that something strange has happened.
The juggler realizing the scourging has ceased and becoming
aware of the silence around him, slowly rises. He sees the
monks are kneeling and all are looking at the church door,
and there above the porch is the Virgin, smiling at him; she
has accepted his offering. Full of joy and praise, the juggler
staggers to the centre and kneels to her. This is all he is
able to do and he falls to the ground and dies in ecstasy.

INDEX